Blairsville Junior High School
Blairsville, Pennsylvania

A TOUR OF THE
WHITE HOUSE WITH
MRS JOHN F. KENNEDY

A TOUR OF THE
WHITE HOUSE WITH
MRS JOHN F. KENNEDY

ILLUSTRATED

by *PERRY WOLFF*

DOUBLEDAY & COMPANY, INC.
GARDEN CITY, NEW YORK
1962

LIBRARY OF CONGRESS CATALOG CARD NUMBER: 62-18608
© 1962 BY COLUMBIA BROADCASTING SYSTEM, INC.
ALL RIGHTS RESERVED
PRINTED IN THE UNITED STATES OF AMERICA

For John Wolff
who has as good a chance
as any American boy.

CONTENTS

INTRODUCTION

THERE have been hundreds of studies of the White House published, ranging from archival tomes to backstairs gossip. More than any other public building in America, the White House stands in the center of our public life, and its slightest change is immediately recorded. It has been fashionable for Presidents to call themselves "the public's chief servant." Such modesty befits campaign oratory, still the American public believes it. To a degree which would be intolerable in the Kremlin, Buckingham Palace, or the Elysées Palace, the White House is an open house. This has given rise to a quantity of documentation concerning the events, people, and furnishings which can bring delight only to a battery of professional historians.

The definitive history of the White House can never be written. The President's house is the President's home as well as the building commanding the Executive Branch of our government. Every day someone moves a chair, or makes a decision, and another increment is added to the story of this building.

Obviously, any history of the President's house must set limits for itself, thus, this book restricts itself to research material gathered for a single television broadcast. It does not pretend to be a definitive record of the house, its events, or its furnishings. This disclaimer is not an attempt to escape responsibility for scholarship. It is sometimes true that by examining the small, the large becomes clearer. Or, in dramatic terms, people don't believe things unless they see them acted out before them.

On a single night in February 1962, almost one-third of a nation saw Mrs John F. Kennedy conduct a television tour of the White House. In an hour more than a hundred thousand electronic pictures were broadcast. During the production period some three hundred unposed photographs were taken. To this selection have been added some historical photographs and documents which could not be used because of restrictions of broadcast time. These figures set the limits on the photographs used in this book.

Our television cameras were in the White House for only three days, and Mrs Kennedy was on set less than seven hours. On the days of taping, in the West Executive Wing the President conducted affairs of State without television present. In the family quarters of the President, private life went on, unrecorded. Mrs Kennedy chose not to show some of the museum rooms of the White House. The President and Mr Charles Collingwood played brief, supporting roles. Otherwise the whole history of the White House reduced itself to the almost irreducible dramatic minimum: one person on stage.

The law of drama stated above was proved again. One woman talked and something profound emerged out of simplicity. The past stirred. Fact invited nuance; a hint became an overtone; a word summoned up an era. A frame of wood and a bit of cloth became a chair, and a chair summoned up a past President and a passage in American history. As the accretion of detail went on, the magic moment of the theater took place. What was happening onstage was far greater than the words being spoken and the woman speaking them.

The mystery of drama can never be explained. The esthetic experience is incapable of reconstruction because it is private, fragmentary, and subjective. Not everyone was bewitched. But for some America stretched out, long and deep, behind the cultured lawns of the White House. Our sins, our excesses, our failures were there dimly, but our strength, goodness, and future were there too—outweighing our defects by far.

A woman spoke for an hour and the White House once more became the central symbol of America.

This book does not pretend so high. This document is an attempt to give some background to Mrs Kennedy's remarks. For instance, later there is the following dialogue:

MR COLLINGWOOD

What's your budget? Where does it come from?

MRS KENNEDY

. . . It's small because everything we do is by private donation . . .

Why she chose to finance the restoration of the White House by private donation instead of by public funds is a story that arises out of American history. The furnishing of the White House has always been a means by which Congress and the public could attack the President. This story is told in more detail in the section titled "The Ground Floor."

Placing footnotes to all of Mrs Kennedy's text would make for uncomfortable reading. The pattern of the book is to weave the author's comments through the emended text of the television program. Some diversionary essays are included. The intention is to trace out inferences, historical background, or anecdotes which stand behind her remarks. A one hour television program contained some 7500 words. This material has been used as a base against which pertinent annotations have been added.

It must be said that these annotations are the author's and not Mrs Kennedy's. To separate her comments from the author's research and opinions, the direct excerpts from the program have been set in larger type throughout the book. The responsibility for everything else including errors, is solely that of the writer.

I am especially grateful to Arthur Bonner who was the associate producer of the broadcast, and who provided calm outlines, background material, and a deep historical knowledge to both book and broadcast. Neither could have been accomplished without him.

Chris Rosenfeld checked the manuscript and provided invaluable source material. She worked closely with Stanley McClure of the Lincoln Museum who has spent many years on White House research. Everyone concerned relied on many sources, not the least of whom was Pamela Turnure, press secretary to Mrs Kennedy, and the White House Curatorial Staff; however this book is not an official publication of the White House nor any governmental organization. The majority of photographs was taken by William Warnecke. Thomas H. Ryan was active in liaison work between the many organizations involved. Milton Beyer and Gabrielle Wachsner typed the manuscript: Mr Beyer provided great help in research involving period furniture. Finally, I should like to thank the officials of CBS News for the total freedom they gave me in preparing the broadcast and writing the book.

THE WALLS OF
THE WHITE HOUSE

"This sketch, made in 1799 before the White House was completed, shows that the original design of the building included an extra floor. George Washington, for reasons of economy, persuaded the architect to eliminate the top floor."

Although the sketch is clearly labeled White House 1799, Mrs Kennedy's remark caused the Library of Congress to investigate the etching, with the unhappy result that the building has now been identified as Blodgett's Hotel.

"This is the final design of the White House, as planned by James Hoban. Mr Hoban won an open competition for the first public building in Washington."

THE basic trouble with the White House is that George Washington was a modest man. In the interests of economy he persuaded the architect to eliminate the top floor of the planned building. From then on, almost every First Lady lost her battle to make the White House a home.

George Washington's modesty was in part political and in part personal. He could never bring himself to call the nation's capital Washington and referred to it as "The Federal City" or "The Capital City." During Washington's term, the presidency had been located in New York and Philadelphia, and his offices were deliberately modest. The grandiose scheme to locate the nation's capital on the banks of the Potomac can only be compared with the present day plans for Brasilia.

The City of Washington was a compromise. Virginia was the most influential of the early states, and the most suspicious of a strong central authority. Economic power lay in the North. The northern bankers wanted the new Federal Government to assume responsibility at par value, for the debts of the former colonies. Alexander Hamilton worked out a compromise; Virginia's leaders accepted the old debts and northern politicians agreed to place the new City of Washington under Virginia's nose, in a district not controlled by any state.

The Executive Mansion was intended as a center of Washington City and the first President undoubtedly had feelings that the planners were overreaching themselves. President Washington was caught between the planners who wanted a large home for the Chief Magistrate, and the suspicions of congressmen who saw the building as a threat to Congress' power. To many, including Washington, the estimated cost of $400,000 seemed excessive. The President's house was a "palace in a forest." There was nothing close to it but swamplands and woods. For all these reasons George Washington—the only President who never lived in the White House—trimmed a floor from the plans.

The basic issue of presidential power was smoldering. The new country had not thrown off the rule of a British king in order to appoint an American king. In the minds of many, the presidency was to be a little more than an honorary position, a central figure for necessary ceremonials, and nothing more. It would be highly injudicious if the First House in the City of Washington should look like a palace. Congress withheld funds, and the Executive Man-

15

sion went up slowly. The construction took ten years, and by the time it was completed part of the house had rotted.

A prize of $500 had been awarded James Hoban whose design won an open competition offered by the District Commissioners of Washington. It would be pretentious to say that the building evoked a storm of controversy. America in 1790 had too much on its mind to engage vigorously in the controversies of architecture. But the reader is invited to view Hoban's final design as if he had never seen the White House before. Hoban had not only to solve the usual problems of building a large house, but he had to do it without offending Congress and the President. At the same time, being a man of some conscience, he obviously wanted to nudge forward the periphery of architecture.

For the most part, Hoban played it safe. There is nothing about the exterior which does not copy manor houses in Ireland, England, and France but Hoban is not to be chastised for copying. Except for the tepee and other Indian dwellings, America had no indigenous architecture. The spirit of Hoban's house is that of a modern European country gentleman's manor of the late eighteenth century. Since the greatest political power in America was concentrated in Virginia, this new house would answer the judgment of the gentlemen of Virginia whose aristocratic tastes were to lead America until Andrew Jackson's time. Hoban knew his audience.

The sole variations Hoban permitted himself are the oval rooms on the south side of the building. The oval rooms were the innovations by which the architect escaped the completely familiar. For the present-day White House visitor who has only a mild interest in architecture, these are the only rooms which call attention to themselves by their form.

Hoban's Georgian house was the one that was built. But there was another design in the competition for the Gold Medal. Thomas Jefferson, who had drawn up the advertisement for the contest Hoban won, submitted an anonymous plan for the Executive Mansion. There is no record of the comments made by the District Commissioners, nor is it known if George Washington paid notice to the plan labeled only "A.Z."

Jefferson's building is worth examining, if only to admire the rare skill of the man. In hindsight, it is a statement concerning the times, the function of the President, and Jefferson's view of democracy.

Jefferson's design echoes Monticello and Italy. Because of the dome it seems larger than Hoban's building. But the windows give away the smallness of the house. In Hoban's final design, the eye moves horizontally; Jefferson forces the eye upward. Hoban's squares off the building functionally; aside from the decorative elements which are pasted on, his house is a well-proportioned box.

16

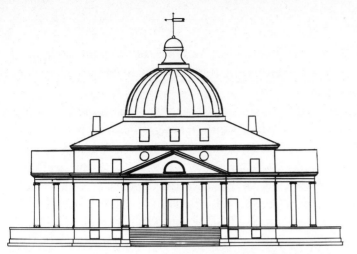

"It wasn't until after Thomas Jefferson's death that it was learned that he had entered a design anonymously into the competition and lost. President Jefferson's design was for a smaller house."

"The British burned the White House on the night of August 24, 1814. The President's house was a blackened ruin and the interior had to be completely rebuilt."

Hoban's walls survived the British burning. Fire-blackened stone from 1814 was discovered during painting and repair in 1945.

Jefferson seemingly wastes space in columns, porches, and a dome. His intent is plain: the President's home is a temple, a monument to the arcadian ideal that underlay Jeffersonian democracy.

The language of architecture is often abstract, and it is tempting to find systems of thought in the arrangement of old or new stones. All buildings are made to be used, and it is difficult to see Andrew Jackson, Abraham Lincoln, or Theodore Roosevelt working at the presidency in such a temple. Jefferson himself had to modify his view of an agricultural democracy. This sketch dates before Jefferson's reluctant acceptance of commerce and trade as forces equal with agriculture in America's life. It is doubtful that President Jefferson would have been comfortable in the design sketched by Thomas Jefferson, Secretary of State.

The Walls of the White House

He was too well-mannered to comment directly to George Washington on Hoban's design, but when Mr Jefferson became President, he did not call on James Hoban. In the remodeling and future planning of the White House, his architect was Benjamin Latrobe. The third President's early feeling about Hoban's house has been quoted as "big enough for two emperors, one Pope, and the Grand Lama."

Benjamin Latrobe complained that the work had been poorly done, and that on a summer's day the smell arising from the open sewer "was not a pleasant prologue to a visit to the President. . . . The south side is ill-proportioned. The north side is undistinguished."

Architect's language occasionally must be translated. What Latrobe meant is that Hoban's design looked like an eighteenth-century English house in a time when the Continent had rediscovered the Greek column. Greek classical architecture had seized center stage at Paris and Versailles some years before the French Revolution. Architectural ideas moved slowly, but Latrobe and Jefferson were strongly influenced by the French adaptations of ancient Greek columns and colonnades. Hoban's original design has at its center four Greek columns, but they are embellishments. Latrobe and Jefferson wanted to emphasize this classic revival even more strongly, and their sketches for the future White House show even the stables and meathouse fronted by Greek columns.

It is not clear how much influence Latrobe had in designing the walls of the White House either before or after the British burned the building. Until recently it has been assumed that Latrobe did the graceful steps on the south side of the building, as well as the porticos and columns on both sides. Current evidence indicates that James Hoban designed both porticos and not Latrobe.

18   In 1829, Hoban wrote a note to Charles Bulfinch, the Architect to the

Government, stating, "In answer to your inquiries, I have to state that a portico to the north front is part of the original plan of the President's House *according to my design*, approved by General Washington." Latrobe's design for the South Portico shows steps coming down the center. The curved steps along the side were built, and they are undoubtedly Hoban's design. Hoban must be credited with both porticos.

All scholarship is difficult, but the piecing together of the early events of the White House is further complicated by the absence of records and the persistence of myth. The British are partially to blame. They burned the White House in late August 1814, thus diminishing the documentation and adding to the fables.

There was enough work for both architects after the burning of the city. Hoban rebuilt the White House. Latrobe finally got his dome and columns when he was commissioned to design the Capitol.

The walls of the President's house were badly burned, and only partly usable in reconstruction. The interior was ready for a reception on New Year's Day, 1818. There is a story that the term White House comes from this period of reconstruction. The walls were painted white to cover the traces of the fire, and the name of the building thus dates from 1818. But there is evidence it was called the White House even earlier. A more reliable story is that it was painted white by Hoban, contrasting with the red brick predominating throughout Georgetown. There is an improbable legend that George Washington named it in honor of Martha Washington's "White House," the home in which the first President and his wife became engaged.

The problem of a name has never been quite settled. At first, because of its size, it was called the President's Palace but anti-monarchial sentiment put the term into disuse. During the time of John Adams, Thomas Jefferson, and James Madison, it was called the President's house. Sometime later it was called the Executive Mansion. The reason for the change is not clear. There is a note from Thomas Jefferson's granddaughter, Martha Randolph, expressing distaste for the term "President's house" because the name is "too plain English to suit modern notions of dignified refinement, for it has been superseded by the more stately appellation of 'Executive Mansion.'" "Stately appellation" or not "Executive Mansion" did not fit the American tongue, though it is used today on appropriation bills. People called it "The White House." In 1902 Theodore Roosevelt made it as official as he could by placing these words on his letterhead.

(One wishes the story would end here, with the simplest of titles. But names wear out, like furniture. Today's visitor to the White House will find matchbooks in the ashtrays on which is written "The President's House.")

George Catlin's sketch of the White House dates after the reconstruction and before the building of the porticos, in 1824 and 1829. Any number of architectural details are incorrect. He had placed a triangle over the doorway instead of an arc, and he had changed the proportions and decorations around all the windows to suit his fancy. There are dozens of other imaginary details which the reader can discover by comparing this with earlier or later sketches. This is the view from the north side, or from Pennsylvania Avenue.

And that leads to another confusion. Which side of the White House is supposed to be the front?

Today, visitors enter from both the north and south sides. Earlier, there was an entrance on the east side. But architectural tidiness demands that one entrance be major. The front door to the building is usually taken as the entrance on the north side, or the side on Pennsylvania Avenue. Yet the picture on the back of the twenty-dollar bill gives prominence to the south side. Chiefs of State enter through the north door—but almost all other visitors enter from the south.

Whether it be Hoban or Latrobe, in 1824 the front door was placed inside the newly erected columns of the South Portico. Until after Lincoln's time this was the major entrance. Visitors mounted the south stairway and stepped into the Blue Room. The trouble is that the large reception hall is on the north side of the building.

It seems absurd to have the front door on one side of the house and the reception hall on the other side. But this was exactly Benjamin Latrobe's intention. He particularly disliked the central hall on the north side of the building. This feature of Georgian houses summoned up the pomp of nobility, with the inferior people waiting in a large hall below a staircase for the lord to enter. Latrobe and Jefferson wanted the White House to appear as a home, directly at the entranceway. Thus, to give an immediate sense of democratic privacy, Latrobe preferred that an entrance be made through the French doors to the Blue Room. The front door got lost in a debate over the architectural meaning of democracy.

The White House was a large building constructed on a ridge overlooking a swamp. The area to the south became a park, and a road was scratched on the north. The city grew around the building. Although Washington, D.C., was a well-planned city, no imagination of the time could envision the growth of America.

The country grew, the President's responsibilities grew—but the size of the White House was fixed. By Andrew Jackson's time the very definition of the presidency demanded that the White House be more than a ceremonial residence for the Chief Magistrate: the President's home had not only to include

"The famous American artist, George Catlin, made this sketch of the North side of the White House, showing it as it must have appeared about 1820."

his family and his offices, as well as a place to receive visitors, but also a kind of General Headquarters in the continuous battle with Congress.

After Jackson the President was no longer a kind of Dean of the College of Electors. He was free to be a force equal to the Congress. Several administrations after Jackson's it became apparent that the White House was beginning to be cramped. Offices began to intrude on the family's private living space. After the Civil War, First Ladies complained, unofficially. Each succeeding administration began to think about enlarging the walls of the building. Grover Cleveland submitted a plan for remodeling, but did not press hard for it. President Cleveland kept the White House as an official residence, but he took a home in Woodley Heights and commuted to work. The next President's wife, Caroline Harrison, spoke up. She was a grandmother, and the head of a large family. She was also the first president of the Daughters of the American Revolution, and she had a keen interest in politics. Mrs Harrison had two major proposals for the walls of the White House. Her first and most radical was that a new Executive Mansion be built on 16th Street. Cooler political heads dissuaded her from making her main attack on this line. Her compromise was a palace with a large wing coming out from each side of the building. A bill for the construction of these Federal-Victorian-Grecian walls was introduced in the House, but failed to be passed. The failure, it might be noted, was not a rejection on esthetic grounds, but because President Harrison was in a patronage dispute, and Congress rebuked him by denying his wife's plans. Congress gallantly gave her money for "modernization . . . electrification . . . and rat extermination."

The Legislative Branch might withstand Mrs Harrison, but Theodore Roosevelt was too formidable an opponent. The Roosevelt clan surveyed the White House on its arrival in Washington, and Alice Roosevelt Longworth (TR's oldest daughter) has related that the cramped White House could only be considered a "*pied à terre* in Washington."

With reason, Theodore Roosevelt attacked the unhealthy, drafty building. He complained of "the peril to health and even to life itself," and this was not simple oratory.

Andrew Jackson's tuberculosis was always at its worst in the White House. William Henry Harrison died of pneumonia contracted on his Inauguration Day and inflamed by the damp and drafty building. It is thought that Zachary Taylor's fatal attack of typhoid was caused by faulty White House plumbing. The relatives of many Presidents complained of illnesses contracted in the President's house. Aside from the Flea Market look of the interior, and the jumbled confusion of offices and private quarters, Theodore Roosevelt meant to have a healthy place for his family.

"The South Portico was added in 1824 and the columns made the White House seem grander. Still, there are sheep grazing, and a vegetable patch on the south lawn."

The South Portico became the ceremonial entrance to the building.

"The North Portico was added in 1829. This was the view from Pennsylvania Avenue."

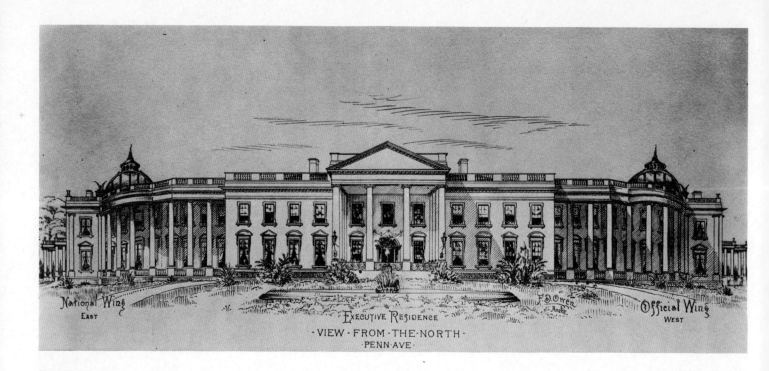

National Wing
EAST

EXECUTIVE RESIDENCE
·VIEW·FROM·THE·NORTH·
PENN·AVE·

F.D.Owen
Arch't

Official Wing
WEST

·VIEW·FROM·THE·SOUTH·
·OF·THE·RESIDENCE·WINGS·
·CONSERVATORY·AND·COURT·

Official Wing
WEST

National Wing
EAST

F.D.Owen
Arch't

24   "Mrs Harrison complained that she had no privacy. She submitted these plans for an enlargement of the building, adding two large wings to contain offices and entertainment rooms. Her plans were not approved."

"This photograph was taken on New Year's Day, 1898. Mr McKinley was President, and he was observing a custom which persisted until Herbert Hoover. New Year's Day was traditionally an 'Open House' when anyone could come to the White House and shake the President's hand. The President's hand was often bandaged for days afterward. The North Portico was illuminated by four gas lamps."

The lamps were removed in 1902, leaving the classic line of the pillars uncluttered.

25

Congress gave the President more than a half-million dollars to redo the walls and the interiors. TR promptly built the West Wing, thus taking the Executive Offices out of the main building.

His command to the architects was: "Discover the design and intention of the original builders and make it comfortable by modern standards . . . It is a good thing to preserve such buildings as historic monuments which keep alive our sense of continuity with the nation's past." The White House was to be redone from top to bottom.

The ground floor was redesigned, and a public entrance was placed under the South Portico. The first floor was reinforced by steel beams, and plumbing and electrical wiring were replaced throughout. The major effort was to be more an exercise in interior decoration than in buttressing or correcting the walls. An elevator was added, and the literature of the time reflected the awe and pride in capital letters: "Roosevelt has succeeded in accomplishing what is officially called The Restoration."

That Theodore Roosevelt had good taste and noble aspiration is undeniable. What is also undeniable is that he misunderstood the principles of contracting and construction. The whole job had to be done between June and October. While parts of the work were well done, a great deal was jerry-built. The timber cutting was impetuous, and the sawdust and bits of wood were left between the old timbers of the second floor and the new flooring above it. The danger of fire was always greatest in the family quarters: had there been even a minor blaze between 1902 and 1948, it could easily have become a national calamity. Although the White House was completely replastered, some ceilings were secured only by driving thousands of nails straight up, through the wet plaster, and then covering the nailheads with another thin coat of plaster.

When the Coolidges moved into the White House the Department of Public Buildings warned that the decaying roof needed extensive repairs. Coolidge coolly commented: "I presume there are plenty of others who would be willing to take the risk of living under that roof." Still the whole third floor was redesigned. In 1927, the old attics were replaced by lighter rooms for guests, servants, sewing, pressing, and storage. A sun deck was installed and the entire floor was fireproofed.

This patchwork added to the risk. The new third floor was supported by trusses but the entire weight of the added structures had to be supported by the old wooden beams of the second floor.

One of the principles of sound engineering is the "safety factor." It is calculated by estimating the dimensions of a beam or truss for the largest possible load. The conservative engineer then designs the member to carry

"The south lawn was a jumble of greenhouses, and the interior was an impossible arrangement of the President's private quarters and Executive Offices."

President Buchanan was the first to add what was stylishly known as a "conservatory" to the west side of the White House. As the demand increased for elaborate floral displays at dinners and receptions, the additions grew larger.

"In 1902 President Roosevelt ordered out the clutter and built the West Wing. This was the first of two temporary extensions which became permanent office wings."

"In 1927, Mrs Coolidge redid the interior and added eighteen rooms to the third floor."

The attic was converted into rooms for guests, servants, sewing, pressing, and storage. A sun deck was installed above the South Portico. The weight of the added rooms almost caused the building to collapse. By 1948 the White House was too dangerous for habitation.

The awnings shaded the South Portico and kept the sun from the Blue Room. President Truman asserted that the awnings marred the grace of the columns.

double or triple the maximum weight. By 1948 the safety factor in certain parts of the White House was less than one. This means that under ordinary use the walls of the White House should have come tumbling down—but they didn't.

Not that there hadn't been hints. In Franklin Roosevelt's time his children heard noises. Ghost stories about the White House were prevalent: creaking noises, knockings at doors, and the rattling of chains. Engineers may stubbornly have insisted on the "safety factor," but in the poetic radicalism and the martial era of FDR many people preferred to believe more in the strength of spirit than in the weakness of walls.

The hints continued when President Truman took office. The great chandeliers in the East Room tinkled—even when there was no breeze. The official documentation says: "President Truman became concerned because of a noticeable vibration in the floors in his study." A commission was appointed to make a stress analysis of the building.

Harry Truman edged into the redesign of the White House by stages. Firstly, he wanted a porch on the south side of the building, and he intended to place it halfway up the pillars on the South Portico. A man of many talents, President Truman had an eye for terrain and architecture. The south lawn slopes upward toward the President's house, and Truman estimated that if he placed a balcony just outside his living quarters, there'd be a pleasant breeze even in the hottest weather. In the 1930s the British Foreign Office officially classified Washington as "sub-tropical climate." The American Midwest had long since solved the problem of evening breezes by the building of porches. The porch is a grand tradition in Midwestern politics and summer life. The Chicago El, snaking its way through the meanest slums in America, finds none so dreamless as to exclude the back-yard porch. The turn-of-the-century status symbol in the Midwest was the porch, and President McKinley centered his campaign on his front porch. It is always called a porch, never a "terrace," "portico," or "balcony," and it is always built of wood.

To those ignorant of Midwestern mores, President Truman's porch was an abomination. The south side of the White House suddenly became sacred, as if the Greeks had built those Ionic columns instead of Latrobe or Hoban. It did not occur to the critics that the South Portico had been added for the same reasons that Midwestern gentlemen give for their whitewashed front porches. The Fine Arts Commission, which technically oversees and guards the esthetics of Washington's monuments, disapproved on artistic grounds. Historians disapproved on historical grounds.

President Truman, who only wanted a little night air, mustered his defenses. On artistic grounds his followers claimed that the Ionic pillars were disproportionately high, and the new porch would break the vertical line as a sort of *trompe l'oeil*. On historical grounds it was pointed out that Georgian homes of the same period as the White House often included similar porches. Finally, though the Fine Arts Commission might disapprove, it could not deny.

President Truman had $10,000 in legal funds at his disposal and he got his porch. The only real casualty was the back of the twenty-dollar bill. The plate had to be redesigned to include the porch.

The area of greatest political danger was in the second plan: the rebuilding of the White House. Shortly after Vice President Truman succeeded President Roosevelt, the new President submitted a modest proposal to Congress which required $1,500,000 for the purpose of making the building safe. A committee headed by Senator Kenneth McKellar turned down the proposal. President Truman wrote an indignant letter to Senator McKellar, and bided his time.

In 1948 Harry Truman was elected President of the United States and as a minor consequence the rebuilding of the White House was assured. The President appointed a Commission to aid him in restoring the walls. It was evident that the original request for $1,500,000 was too modest. Some $5,400,000 would be needed. President Truman saw to it that the Chairman of the Commission on the Renovation of the Executive Mansion was the same man who was the Chairman of the Senate Appropriations Committee—Senator Kenneth McKellar.

Not only engineers build safety factors into their plans.

The Chairman of the House Appropriations Committee showed signs of balking. Representative Clarence Cannon had made his reputation as "a slow man with a buck." He pointed out that by tearing down the whole house, including the walls, at least a million dollars could be saved. Otherwise tunnels some twenty-five feet deep would have to be dug under the existing walls and foundations, and then filled with cement as underpinning. Clearly a costly, laborious procedure. Representative Cannon found himself in the unpopular position of the man who would go down in history as the destroyer of the White House walls. After dutifully registering his protest, he quickly gave way.

The accompanying photographs and text by Mrs Kennedy tell the main outlines. During the four-year reconstruction, many of these photographs were treated as classified documents, and were unavailable to the press. One can debate the merits of such censorship, but those who restricted the photographs had decided that the White House was a central symbol of the American experience. They thought it would have been shocking to show the demolition and reconstruction before the symbol was restored.

The same caution had been exercised before the major work began. Public dignitaries, journalists, and other potential decision makers had been given

"In 1948 President Truman became concerned because the floor of his study was vibrating."

After President Truman was re-elected, he returned to Washington to find that the massive ceiling of the East Room was propped up by an improvised scaffold. The Trumans were moved to Blair House, an official guest house.

"An investigation was held and the structural weakness of the White House became immediately apparent."

31

guided tours of the shell of the old building. The creaking of the walls could be heard with a stethoscope. The soot stains from the British burning were still present, and the hastiness of the earlier palliative repairs was evident.

The building was air conditioned, fireproofed, restressed, equipped with outlets for television cables, and jammed in every way with the comforts of the middle twentieth century. At the same time, the interior and exterior architecture was made to conform with the past—or as much as could be discovered and approved.

President Truman had one more plan—redecoration of the interior. For reasons which will be discussed later, the furnishings of the White House flowed in and out the doors with each administration. Harry Truman wanted to fill the White House with antiques from significant periods in White House history, or with memorabilia of previous Presidents. He asked for an additional half-million dollars, and Congress promptly vetoed the request. His appropriation was the usual $50,000.

Thus the faded, sometimes tattered hangings came back into the new house, and were supplemented by other phenomena of the middle twentieth century: copies of old pieces, sometimes called "Louis l'Hotel" by indignant interior decorators. The Red Room, for example, was furnished by a New York department store in imitation Louis XV style. Imitation was bad enough; Louis XV was worse. Louis Quinze was King of France before the United States was founded. The best that could be done was to group, here and there, the authentic pieces.

By March 1952, the walls of the White House were secured. It seems reasonable to assume that the building will stand firmly for another century.

In this rapid summary are the hints of the problems of the interior. The debates between Congress and the President; the problems of living, working, and receiving guests; all took place within the walls, and are hinted at by the walls.

Yet it is a good thing to begin with the building itself. Unlike temples, fortresses, and palaces, each of which has been built as a monument to a purpose, or as the architecture for an attitude, the function of the White House has never quite been settled. It is a home, an office, a museum, and the only substitute we have for a palace.

All this is unsettling only to the professional architect, particularly those who want form to follow function. It is just as well that James Hoban copied the walls of James Gibb's "Design for a Gentleman's House." What form could foresee the functions of America? The house would have to be designed for a federation of states that became one nation; a continental power, and then a leading world power. It would have to function well for old widowers,

"The White House was taken apart like a jigsaw puzzle. The pieces were marked and stored away."

A workman is removing the Joliet stone from the floor of the entrance hall.

The large ornamental design at the center of the East Room ceiling was first loosened, then lowered carefully to the wooden scaffolding. Later it was decided to install a simpler design.

young brides, childless families, and whole broods like the Harrisons and the Roosevelts. One room would have to function for marriages and caskets, two thousand visitors a day, chamber music recitals, balls, and ju-jitsu exhibitions.

The White House has had to contain a distillate of the American experience. No architect could foresee this function.

It is because of this haphazardness that the White House is a great building. Its greatness has been given to it by American lives. It is no jewel of architecture, cold and efficient, or monumental and anachronistic. What it is has been placed into it by American lives. In today's age, when most new buildings are built by corporations for corporations (or corporation presidents), the White House has the look of humanity. It was built for men, by men.

The Walls of the White House

34

Mrs Kennedy in the ground floor office of the Curator of the White House. The room is attic, cellar, and workroom all in one. Donations and purchases for the White House are received and examined here.

"It would have been easier and less expensive to demolish the whole **building**, but the White House is so great a symbol to Americans that the exterior walls were retained."

"The whole inside was scooped out. Only the exterior walls were left standing. Steel beams were rigged in the interior."

The new steel bracing was set on concrete piers as deep as 27 feet below ground level. This added depth provided room below the ground floor for public toilets, mechanical facilities, and storage.

"It was a little difficult to get the new steel beams through the windows designed by Mr Hoban in 1790."

"Then, piece by piece, the interior of the President's house was put back together."

The reconstruction offered an opportunity to make some needed changes in interior decoration. The chandeliers in the East Room were reduced in size and hung a few inches higher. Small, candlelike bulbs were installed with a dimmer device which controls the intensity of the lighting.

The dark oak panels installed by McKim, Mead & White in 1902 were put back in place and painted a pale green. In this picture one panel is painted as a guide for the final color of the room.

"The exterior views were exactly those which Americans had seen throughout this century except for the balcony on the South Portico, which President Truman added in 1946."

THE GROUND FLOOR

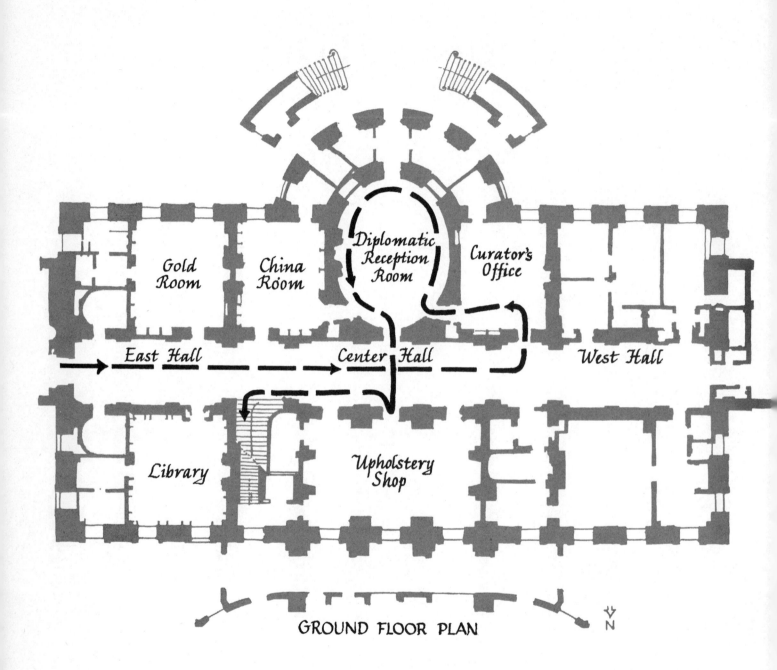

Gold Room

China Room

Diplomatic Reception Room

Curator's Office

East Hall

Center Hall

West Hall

Library

Upholstery Shop

GROUND FLOOR PLAN

N

The broken line indicates the path of Mrs Kennedy during the television program.

THE ground floor of the White House was once a basement. With variations its story is that of utility rooms throughout American history. Yet, like everything else in the White House, it contains the echoes of the past and it reflects the changes in American life.

The ground floor of James Hoban's late eighteenth-century house was intended for the leisurely, uncluttered life of a manor house. Water came from wells and sanitary facilities were outhouses. Gentlemen had their kitchens out of sight and the architect grouped the servants' quarters, wine cellars, and general storage facilities on the ground floor. Hoban's house was meant to be lived in by one aristocratic family and a few distinguished guests. All were to enter the building in small numbers. In 1800 Washington had a population of some 3500—Hoban could not have known that his house would have to accommodate 15,000 people in a single day. Nor could he have foreseen electric cables, television outlets, steam and gas pipes, and a heliport on the south lawn. The changes in the ground floor have been the most radical departures from Hoban's original themes.

The architect designed for gentlemen who liked to have a view of the terrain. In his day the White House overlooked an insignificant stream called the Tiber. This creek wound its way southward through the marshes that led to the Potomac. Though the vista was a fine one, the ground floor was always damp. During Martin Van Buren's administration Senator Thomas Hart Benton's daughter wrote:

"The house was so badly underdrained that in all long rains the floors of the kitchens and cellars were actually under water."

As the wooden floors rotted, they were covered with another layer of wood. In turn, each succeeding layer was recovered. When Mrs Benjamin Harrison finally tore up the damp, smelly floor, in places she found five successive layers of wood piled atop each other, like geological strata. Only the cockroaches appreciated the ground floor.

By Mrs Harrison's time the utilitarian glories of modern civilization had edged into the White House. Boilers, pipes, conduits, and cables were scattered through the ground floor. The electric cables were faultily insulated, and were tacked on the ceilings.

41

Hoban designed a large kitchen where cooks prepared dinners in pots, pans, and kettles suspended by cranes and hooks over wood fires. The architect's functional plans became quickly outdated. In 1850 Millard Fillmore tried to improve the kitchen by adding a modern stove, but his cook was upset by its futuristic design. The flues and draughts were beyond him. The cook appealed to Fillmore who made a trip to the Patent Office where the President personally inspected the model. He then taught the cook how to use the stove and peace was restored to the kitchen.

The Ground Floor

In the 1890s Mrs Benjamin Harrison moved the main kitchen to the northwest side of the ground floor where it has remained.

The most awkward part of Hoban's plan was that of placing the visitors' entrance one floor above the ground. If Hoban could not foresee the long lines of tourists, neither could he have seen the growth of the official receiving lines which the President's house would have to accommodate. Until 1902 the architect's design forced the official and unofficial visitors to enter by the first floor and not the ground floor. The result was "disagreeable and unsightly" according to an official of the time. Hats, coats, robes, and other impedimenta were strewn around the state parlors and formal rooms. The receiving lines of foreign and national dignitaries were interrupted and cluttered by makeshift checking facilities.

Theodore Roosevelt's restoration placed a visitors' entrance on the ground floor. A remodeled door under the South Portico permitted guests to enter an oval room called the Diplomatic Reception Room. Adjacent rooms were used for coats and hats. Three other rooms were created which later became known as the Library and the Gold and China Rooms.

The Library is little more than a setting. Since Theodore Roosevelt, Presidents have kept their books on the second floor, in the family quarters. In 1952, when the first television tour of the White House was broadcast, President Truman remarked that he had more books in his upstairs library than were in the official library on the ground floor.

The Gold and China Rooms can also be used as check rooms, but there has always been an effort to make them into minor museums. The China Room has traditionally displayed the porcelains of earlier Presidents. The Gold Room displays vermeil objects which have been valued at one million dollars.

The rest of the rooms on the floor are utilitarian. Hoban's kitchen became a storage room. When movies became more popular, it was turned into a small theater. Later, a private movie theater was placed in the East Executive Wing and the room became the control booth for radio broadcasts from the White House. It is now a general utility room which on the day of broadcast was being used as an upholstery shop.

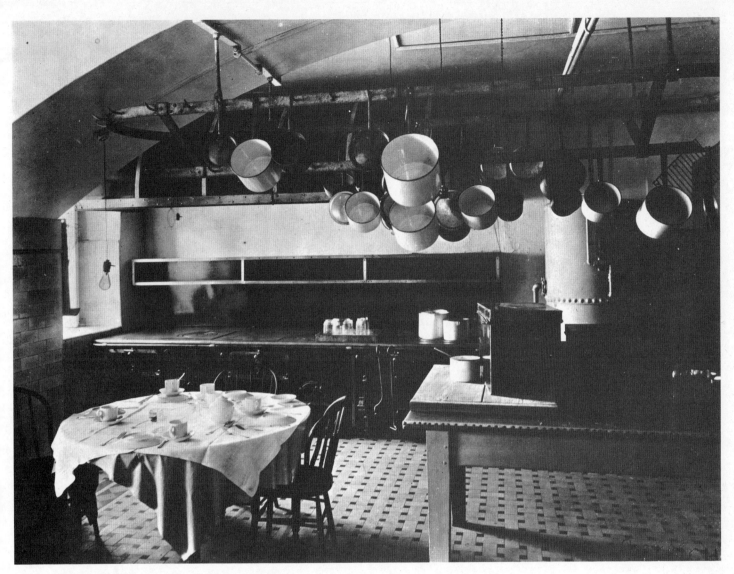

The kitchen of the White House, 1901.

Housekeeping rooms fill the west side of the ground floor. There is a small suite of offices for the President's personal physician, and an office for the housekeeper. Opposite is the kitchen. An elevator is available for the use of the President's family and for his personal visitors who are carried directly to the family quarters, two stories above the ground floor.

Presidents and First Ladies pass quickly through the ground floor and historians quickly pass over this utilitarian area. But this is the first interior seen by today's tourist. It triggers the first impression and the first emotional response. Although the ground floor is only prelude, and although the hushed, central corridor recalls the lobbies of theaters and public buildings, one is, after all, in the home of the President of the United States. Though the ghosts on the ground floor are of recent vintage, the tour into the past begins here.

The sense of history is quickly coupled with a second impression: the building seems small. The powers of the President and the breadth of America are so vast that most visitors expect the White House to be larger than it is. However forewarned the visitor may be, however well he understands that the President's house was built in simpler, smaller times, the first impression is a shock. The ground floor destroys the preconception of a palace. The most common confusion equates size with grandeur. The ground floor has neither.

From Hoban's time to today, the ground floor has traditionally been devoted to the administration and housekeeping of the White House. Mrs Kennedy had these matters on her mind when she began to speak.

The Ground Floor

44

The Curator's Office
... and Mrs Kennedy's Plans

Mrs Kennedy and Charles Collingwood in the ground-floor Curator's Office.

An extensive outline of the program was prepared in consultation with Mrs Kennedy and her aides. Before each scene she discussed her movements and commentary so that the cameras would be prepared to follow her actions. While the tour was being recorded on videotape, she spoke from memory, without the use of a teleprompter or other visual aids.

The scene is the Curator's Office—once a check room, once a map room in which Franklin Roosevelt followed the progress of World War II.

(*Mrs Kennedy and Charles Collingwood enter*)

The Ground Floor

MR COLLINGWOOD

Mrs Kennedy, I want to thank you for letting us visit your official home. This is obviously the room from which most of the work on it is directed.

MRS KENNEDY

Yes, it's attic and cellar all in one. Since our work started we've received hundreds of letters every day. This is where we evaluate all the finds and see if we want to keep them—if they'll fit into our budget.

MR COLLINGWOOD

Before we look at any of the changes you've made, what's your basic plan?

MRS KENNEDY

Well, I really don't have one because I think this house will always grow and should. It just seemed to me such a shame when we came here to find hardly anything of the past in the house, hardly anything before 1902. I know that when we went to Colombia, the Presidential Palace there had all the history of that country in it—where Simon Bolivar was—every piece of furniture in it has some link with the past. I thought the White House should be like that.

MR COLLINGWOOD

Can you make these changes according to your own personal taste and desires?

46

Mrs Kennedy and the director, Frank Schaffner, in the Curator's Office. No attempt
was made to clear up the clutter.

47

MRS KENNEDY

No. I have a committee which has museum experts and government officials and private citizens on it. And then everything we do is subject to approval by the Fine Arts Commission.

MR COLLINGWOOD

The Ground Floor   What's your budget? Where does it come from?

MRS KENNEDY

It's small. Everything we do is by private donation, and every time we find an object we want, we have to search for a donor. It's very slow. That way, a lot of things we would like to get slip away from us.

MR COLLINGWOOD

Suppose you and your committee were to acquire some of the things that are in this room. What happens when the next president's wife comes into the White House?

MRS KENNEDY

If they did not want it in the past, they could sell it, throw it out—do anything with it they wanted. Then a law was passed last spring—which we asked to have passed—whereby everything that's given to, or bought by the White House, becomes part of its permanent collection. If a future First Family doesn't want it, it goes to the Smithsonian where it will be taken care of.

(*They exit Curator's Office*)

The above exchange is an object lesson in modesty, history, and American politics. Today's America has an interest in antiques which is a relatively new phenomenon. It seems astounding that any artifact which has ever been in the President's house could be junked, or casually sold, or auctioned. If the law Mrs Kennedy discusses had been passed in the early nineteenth century, the

White House would be filled with objects of priceless historical value. But—with certain exceptions—nineteenth-century Presidents and First Ladies had no interest in antiques.

The White House has always been a place of deeds, and not décor. Within minor limitations, any President who was able to wrangle sufficient funds from Congress could have the house redecorated in any manner that pleased him. The President and his wife were permitted to get rid of any furniture they didn't like and redecorate according to fancy, whim, or taste. The flow of objects in and out of the White House was continuous.

Until recently, the White House was always furnished in modern. It would not have occurred to Dolley Madison to furnish in Jacobean or Louis XIV, nor would later Presidents have chosen anything but what the better people were using at the time. The struggle was to keep the building up-to-date.

With certain rare exceptions, White House families had only a temporary attachment to the furnishings. The house was something like a private hotel; each family knew it had checked in for multiples of four years. No one feels strong attachment to furniture which is only rented. Like a good hotel, when the pieces looked shabby they were thrown out and new items were moved in. A torrent of furniture has poured through the White House. As the years progressed the décor became aimless and various plans were proposed for permanent redecoration.

Mrs Kennedy's plan for the restoration of the White House echoes the alarms of earlier First Ladies. In April 1881 President Garfield and his wife Lucretia went to the Library of Congress to discover something about the history of the Executive Mansion. Mrs Garfield hoped to furnish their new home in a manner which would recall its past, but the Garfields found that research material was sparse and that intensive scholarship would be required. The Garfields did not have time to pursue the matter; the President was shot three months later and died.

From 1881 to 1923 there was no effort to retrieve presidential memorabilia, or to protect the few antiques still in the White House. Then interest in historical furniture revived. During President Coolidge's time, his wife planned to furnish the President's house with genuine pieces dating from the period in which the White House was designed. Grace Coolidge visited government warehouses, hoping to find antiques of historic interest. Aside from a single chair which reputedly belonged to Andrew Jackson, almost nothing of value was found. Mrs Coolidge prevailed on Congress to pass a resolution authorizing the White House to accept gifts of early American furniture. Although she furnished the Green Room with donations, she did not receive many pieces of value.

49

Her successor, Lou Hoover, picked up the thread. She commissioned a friend to write a history of the White House and its furnishings. Mrs Hoover found some small items: a bust of Van Buren and a desk Lincoln used at the Soldiers' Home. These were brought into the house. In Monroe's law office in Fredericksburg, Virginia, Mrs Hoover found some pieces which she thought Monroe had used in the White House. When she could not purchase them she had copies made and tried to create a Monroe Room on the second floor.

The Ground Floor
President Truman suggested that a committee be formed to acquire antique and historic furniture for the building. The committee could not operate efficiently because its funds depended on Congressional appropriation at a time when President Truman and Congress were not on the best of terms.

The problems of scholarship are difficult, but the problem of money has always been overwhelming. Congress has been alternately generous or parsimonious. Aside from Congressional appropriation, the traditional means of getting money for new furniture has been to sell or auction off the old pieces. Major auctions have taken place during the administrations of Van Buren, Buchanan, Johnson, and Arthur.

The most celebrated auction was in 1882. Chester Arthur disliked the shabby White House he had inherited from James Garfield. He was a dapper widower who had a personal valet, and he refused to move into the White House until it met his tastes. "I will not live in a house looking this way," he declared. "If Congress does not pay for it . . . I will go ahead and pay for it out of my own pocket." He swept up 24 wagonloads of furniture and auctioned all the furniture from the East and Green Rooms, and part of the Red Room. Carpets, curtains, chandeliers, beds, sofas, chairs, pots, and pans went under the hammer. The auction was so complete that newspapers reported the sale of "a rat trap that caught the rat that ate the suit that belonged to Mr Lincoln." Furniture dating back to Andrew Jackson disappeared—and Victorian, machine-made pieces replaced hand-carved antiques.

Reliance on Congressional appropriations and auctions has always kept the White House in a condition between the fairly respectable and the downright shabby. Mrs Kennedy's plan to finance redecoration by private donation is an attempt to escape total dependence on government funds or auctions. The appointment of a curator and a research staff gives some guarantee of historical accuracy and of fair market prices for antiques. The inclusion of the Smithsonian Institution as the repository for any furniture shipped out of the White House gives future First Ladies the freedom to change the White House as they wish. But there are two tricky problems: politics and style.

The style of furnishings was not much of a problem for most earlier First

Families. It has already been remarked that nineteenth-century families decorated the building in whatever was up-to-date. At the beginning of this century there was a vogue for reproductions of English and French furniture of the late eighteenth century. The pieces brought in during Theodore Roosevelt's time were copies of furniture popular in France around 1800. But as America found a sense of history, and as the White House evolved, it seemed improper to use copies of anachronistic pieces. Genuine pieces—antiques—were the answer.

Antiques of what period? Mrs Kennedy's committee tried to find an answer. The White House could hardly be frozen into one period and still recall the whole continuity of the nation's past. Unlike Mount Vernon which is a shrine to Washington, or Monticello which reflects Jefferson's taste, the styles of the White House ought to reflect the evolution of American history. But pieces could not be chosen from every period: between 1860 and 1900 for instance, the White House was glutted with the worst of machine-made Victorian. Unlike a museum, the President's house must be used daily.

The antiques have been chosen by two standards: objects which personally belonged to past Presidents were to be included; and groupings were made of the best styles of the nineteenth-century American furniture. The Red, Blue, and Green Rooms become specific collections of definite eras in American cabinetmaking. The Lincoln Room centers on one President. Other rooms combine both criteria.

Although Mrs Kennedy credits commissions, curators, and experts, like everything to do with style in the White House a final authority must rule. It seems apparent that she is willing to take the risk.

The greater risk is political. Almost nothing that enters the White House is invulnerable to Washington's favorite game. Congressional appropriations often have risen and fallen with presidential popularity. From dogs to décor, everything new in the President's house has been scrutinized for possible political meaning. Although Mrs Kennedy's plan releases the building from the lower level of a political scrap for money, it is not politics-proof. Nonpartisan societies, commissions, curators, and experts notwithstanding, a donation of furniture or cash can still be regarded in the professional political mind as a donation to the President. Some future donation will undoubtedly be considered part of a dark plot to influence the President, no matter how much high-minded insulation is provided by cultural experts. A refusal to donate objects (as when the DAR recently refused two matching chairs for the Blue Room) may raise equally dark equations. Though Mrs Kennedy has been studiously nonpolitical, the risk is still there. Again, she seems willing to take it.

51

The furniture dates from the Revolutionary period. The chairs are sometimes called "Martha Washington," but this is the name given to a style of Federal chair, rather than indicating that Mrs Washington owned them. The sofa is the Hepplewhite line. The round table is a Pembroke, or drop leaf, breakfast table. The oval rug has a border encompassing fifty stars and seals.

. . . and some wallpaper

Before the recording of each scene, Mrs Kennedy waited for the positioning of lights and cameras.

The early American furniture in this room was a gift to the Eisenhowers from the National Society of Interior Decorators. This group donated the wallpaper to Mrs Kennedy. Printed in 1834 by Jean Zuber, these French made papers are a fanciful study of famous American scenes. The wallpaper shows a European view of America in the nineteenth century.

53

(They enter the Diplomatic Reception Room)

MR COLLINGWOOD

What is the Diplomatic Reception Room used for aside from receiving diplomats?

MRS KENNEDY

This is the room people see first when they come to the White House. Everyone who comes to a State Dinner comes through it and leaves by it, so I think it should be a pretty room.

This is wallpaper that was printed in France about 1834. It's all scenes of America: Indians, Niagara Falls, New York Harbor, West Point, Boston Harbor, and Natural Bridge. These wing chairs are rather interesting because they're American, as is all the furniture in this room. They were made in New England, about 160 years ago. Mrs Eisenhower brought all this superb furniture into the room, we added the wallpaper.

MR COLLINGWOOD

Speaking of making things, I understand you've turned one part of this floor into a furniture shop. Is that right?

(They leave the Diplomatic Reception Room, cross corridor and enter Upholstery Room)

MRS KENNEDY

That's true . . . we have an upholstery shop here where we do all our furniture restoring and upholstery . . . And also in this room we have three ladies on loan to us from the National Park Service who catalogue every single item in the White House so we'll be sure that nothing is lost track of again. All donors will be given credit in a book that everyone can see.

(*They exit upholstery shop and walk down corridor*)

MR COLLINGWOOD

There are a lot of other rooms in this part of the White House. Are there any that we really need to see?

The Ground Floor

MRS KENNEDY

Well, there's the China Room, the Gold Room, and the Library which isn't finished yet. I think the first two are so well known that it would be better to go upstairs where the rooms there are of so much greater interest.

(*They start up the stairs to the first floor*)

Detail of Zuber wallpaper in Diplomatic Reception Room: an American Indian dance.

56

Niagara Falls: Nineteenth-century Europeans were impressed by the scenic wonders of the eastern part of the United States—just as modern Europeans are by the scenery of the West.

58 Natural Bridge, Virginia, fits neatly between two of the four doors in the Diplomatic Reception Room.

Cadets march on the plain of West Point with the Hudson River in the background. There are eight wall sconces in the room—all of early American design with hurricane shades.

59

60 This is the Diplomatic Reception Room as it was from 1952 until 1960. Portraits of First Ladies hung on the walls. The center figure is Mrs Theodore Roosevelt.

The upholstery shop on the ground floor.

Originally this was Hoban's kitchen. It became successively a storage room, a movie theater, and a broadcasting control room. Across the corridor is the Diplomatic Reception Room and the door leading to the south lawn.

61

THE FIRST FLOOR

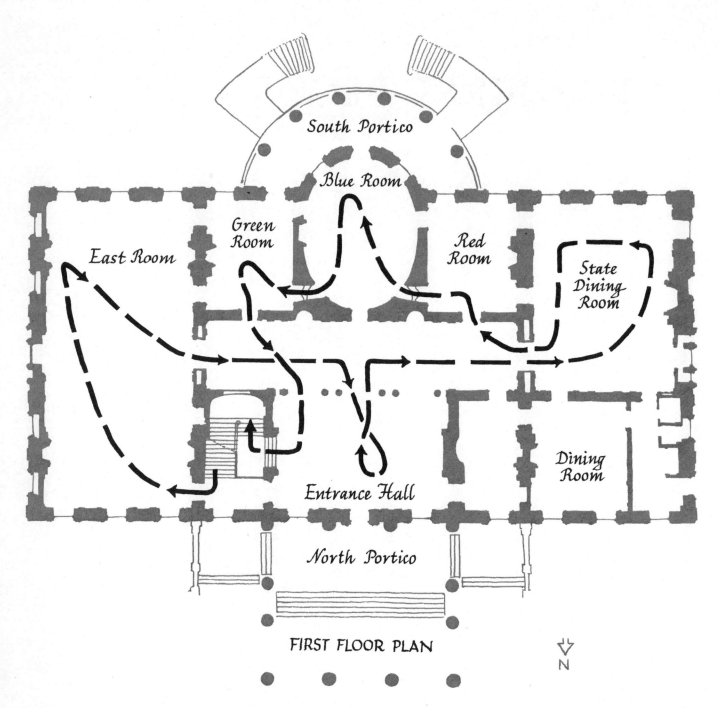

South Portico

Blue Room

Green Room

East Room

Red Room

State Dining Room

Entrance Hall

Dining Room

North Portico

FIRST FLOOR PLAN

N

The broken line indicates the path of Mrs Kennedy during the television program.

THE first floor of the White House is the essence of the President's home. It is that part of the building which almost fits the visitor's preconceptions of the White House, and it is the most direct link with the past.

The reader who studies the floor plan will see that the over-all dimensions are small. An area of 80 feet by 160 feet is subdivided into six major rooms, a corridor, and an entrance hall. These rooms and this floor space serve the ceremonial purposes of the President of the United States.

For the same ceremonial functions, the President of France has the chateaux of Versailles and Rambouillet—hundreds of rooms for official entertainments. The Queen of England uses six hundred rooms of Buckingham Palace for ceremony and family life. There is a story that when Hollywood faithfully reproduced the first floor of the White House for a biography of a President, the director could not fit half his extras into the set.

The furnishings are not elaborate. There are no jeweled settings, no great carpets, no high, vaulted ceilings, nor elaborate carvings and paintings. A man and his family live here: the rooms say clearly that he is a President and not a king. Europeans see this immediately. Emil Ludwig once wrote:

"The White House is not splendid enough for a castle but more striking than a private home. The patrician aspect of this house is at once almost princely and yet private. One would say that here lives the father of a country."

The plan shows a dining room smaller than many serving private homes and embassies in Washington. The central hall leads to the Blue Room flanked by the Red and Green Rooms: all are so modest as to be called parlors. The largest is the East Room. Its length is the width of the building, and its width is a quarter of the White House's length. Such simple fractions are themselves a reminder of the Federal period in which the house was built. The proportions of the room repeat the same eighteenth-century theme: elegance is the fruit of rationality. To the modern visitor, the sole sign of luxury is the height of the ceiling—but a ceiling twenty-two feet high measures more the poverty of our age than the extravagance of earlier times.

The East Room
. . . and ceremony

"The East Room was originally intended as an audience room—something like the throne room in European palaces. Used for funerals, weddings, meetings with American Indians and foreign dignitaries, the East Room gradually became associated in the American mind as the place for the grand events in the White House."

66

The Japanese ministers were received by President Buchanan during the brilliant Washington social season of 1860, a year before the Civil War. They brought as gifts "saddles beautifully embroidered and embossed in gold and silver, bed curtains and screens, two princely swords, kimonos, lacquered ware, writing cases and a superb tea set inlaid with pearls and gold valued at $3000." The reception in the East Room was watched by invited guests who were not presented to the Japanese dignitaries. Only the wives of the cabinet members and Harriet Lane, President Buchanan's niece and hostess, were considered of high enough rank to be presented to the ministers during a private reception in the Blue Room.

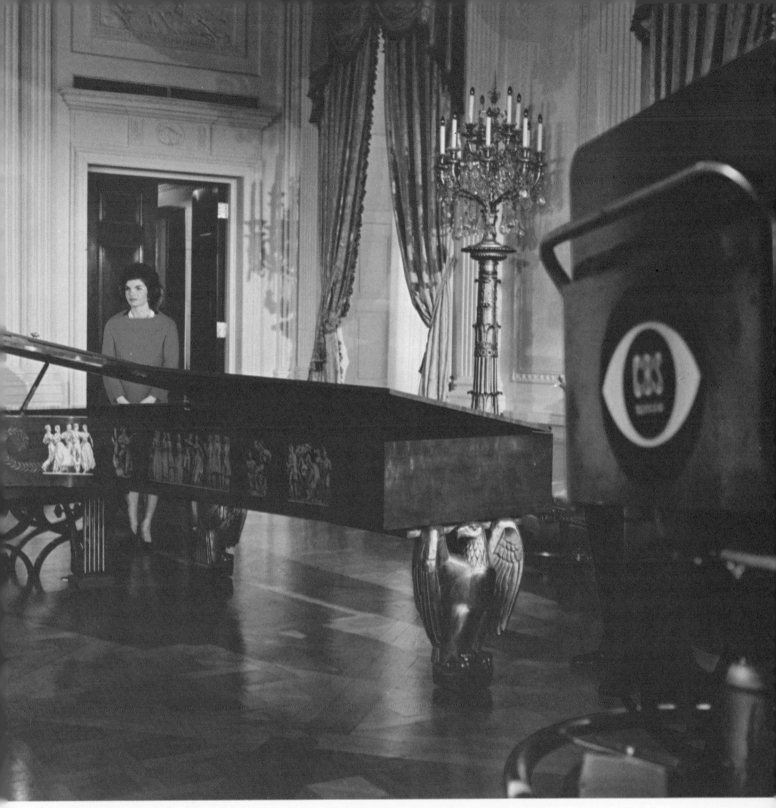

Mrs Kennedy waits while the most complicated shot of the television program is planned. The mirrors in the East Room reflected lights and cameras during her move, but she remained calm while a dozen technicians worked.

The design of the piano is often attributed to Franklin Roosevelt. President Roosevelt merely gave approval to the plans of Eric Gugler of New York. The eagle supports are gilded. The panels on the side represent American folk dancers.

"The artists made the East Room seem larger and larger and raised the ceiling higher and higher, until it resembled the Hall of Mirrors at Versailles."

Again, President Buchanan, and a formal receiving line. Buchanan's taste ran heavily toward Victorian reproductions of Louis XV furnishings. His social receptions grew more elaborate as his political leadership crumbled.

Late eighteenth-century America may have revolted against kings and palaces, but not all ceremonial forms could be cast aside. In the first years of the new republic the political role of the President was not well defined. His ceremonial position was even less clear. The strong anti-monarchial sentiment reflected itself in Congressional reluctance to provide money to finish the East Room. The large size echoed the throne rooms of royalty, and although it was recognized that the President would need one grand room for large social gatherings, the East Room was the last room to be finished. When President John Adams occupied the White House in 1800, Abigail Adams wrote:

"If they will put me up some bells and let me have wood enough to keep fires, I design to be pleased. We have not the least fence, yard or other convenience and the great unfinished audience room I make a drying-room of, to hang the clothes in."

After the British burned the White House, the East Room was used as an enormous storage hall. It was temporarily furnished for the marriage of James Monroe's daughter.

John Quincy Adams finished the East Room walls although he did not provide furniture for it. He was a President who had trouble ridding himself of aristocratic forms. His political enemies charged that the President left the sofas and chairs deliberately unfinished so that visitors could not sit in his presence. There may have been some truth to the charge, but there is a more likely cause in the political struggles between Adams and Congress. John Quincy Adams wanted the East Room finished, but he also wanted to see the North Portico added. In 1826 a senator attended a reception at the White House and was appalled by the condition of the East Room. He promptly persuaded his fellow lawmakers to vote enough money to finish both the East Room and the North Portico.

At the same time President Adams spent $84.50 of his own money on a billiard table and a chess set. He was promptly attacked in Congress for introducing gaming to the White House and called "a corrupter of the youth of the nation." In great disdain, Adams spent only $6000 of the $25,000 which Congress had given him. He papered the East Room a "fine lemon color," brought in enough temporary furniture for a ball in 1828 and left the White House with its East Room still unfurnished.

The room was finished in 1829 under Andrew Jackson. Jackson's tastes were aristocratic. He spent $10,000 on the room without worrying about charges of monarchial pomp. Three gilt chandeliers; bronze tables in gilded woods with Italian marble tops; Italian marble fireplaces; imported silken draperies. Jackson's elegance belied his reputation as the President of "King Mob." Jackson saw to it that Adams' sofas and chairs were covered so that visitors ". . . won't be kept standing upon their legs as they do before kings and emperors and as practiced by Mr. Clay's President . . ." (Jackson so disliked Adams that he would not call him by name.)

One of the minor delights forgotten by our century is the promenade. During the last century every sensible architect provided large, elegant, but sparsely furnished rooms for ladies to show themselves and their clothes. The East Room was naturally suited for seeing and being seen—the essence of the promenade. A description of the East Room in Polk's time reads:

"The great amusement of the evening now commences; all before has been merely preparatory. This popular court pastime consists in solemnly promenading around the room in pairs. Senators, Ministers, Congressmen, mechanics, clerks and would-be clerks are there, leading ladies belonging to every stage in society—from the fashionable belle of the higher circles to the more fashionable seamstress. Solemnly and without pause, they perform their slow gyrations, while a group of young men in the center survey their motions, quizzing their dresses and appearance. The President enters. The noise increases, the complimenting and bowing go on worse than ever; the promenading ceases."

The East Room became the center of the Washington social season. It received greater crowds and the furnishings wore out more quickly. Mary Lincoln tried to add to its glories. She sent a Philadelphia decorator to Paris for wallpaper. She also ordered a new carpet from Glasgow, made in a single piece and patterned with fruits, flowers, wreaths, and bouquets. Her taste was for the heavily ornamented and she spent most of her appropriation on the East Room.

Like everything she touched, luck was against her. During the Civil War the crowds surged through the building, and a new fad had broken out—the taking of souvenirs. After an 1864 reception the newspapers wrote that paper had been pulled from the walls, large pieces of brocade and damask had been slashed away and the heavy cords and tassels of the draperies stolen. The souvenir hunters brought scissors and knives and snipped flowers from the upholstery to use in making pincushions. One lady fainted when caught. Even the stationing of guards did not help. A guard wrote: "The White House looked as if a regiment of rebel troops had been quartered there—with permission to forage."

69

"Here the dignitaries of the Civil War are greeted by President Lincoln. Nobody smiles, and everybody but President Lincoln is frozen upright. The artist left a respectful amount of carpet showing; Mary Lincoln had spent a lot of money for the carpet and her husband was angry."

Mrs Lincoln, who stands at the President's side, ordered the carpet from Glasgow. She also imported French velvet wallpaper, patterned in crimson, garnet, and gold. The East Room draperies came from France and Switzerland. Her purchases cost more than the amount appropriated by Congress for furnishing the White House. When President Lincoln learned of this, he exclaimed: "I'll pay it out of my own pocket first. It would stink in the nostrils of the American people to have it said that the President of the United States had approved a bill over-running an appropriation of $20,000 for flub-dubs for this damned old house, when the soldiers cannot have blankets." Eventually the government paid the bill.

"And this—the earliest photograph—is the East Room in President Johnson's time."

Mary Lincoln's expensive carpet and other decorations were ruined by heavy usage during the Civil War. President Johnson's daughter, Martha Patterson, replaced the carpet and repaired most of the furniture.

71

After the Civil War, the East Room was described:

"Soldiers had wandered unchallenged through the entire suites of parlors. The East Room, soiled and dirty, was filled with vermin. Guards had slept upon the sofas and carpets till they were ruins."

The First Floor

Andrew Johnson's administration cleaned out the room and made a relatively simple restoration. But the major work was done by General Grant who called in the Army Engineers.

The rooms on the floor above the East Room were the executive offices of the President, and were filled with heavy files and furniture. A report to Congress noted: "Many of the floor and roof timbers are in a state of decay. One large ceiling fell last year, fortunately when the room was unoccupied . . ." Grant's Army Engineers probably thought columns were necessary to buttress the ceiling. This is perhaps the only excuse for the garish Greek columns and ornate beams that filled the East Room until Theodore Roosevelt's renovation.

During the late Victorian period the potted palm became a symbol of elegance. It is not known whether their profusion in the East Room was a result of fashion, or a desperate attempt to hide an embarrassing décor.

Though Theodore Roosevelt's restoration is credited to the firm of McKim, Mead & White, the leading spirit was Charles Follen McKim. As one of America's leading architects he tried to lead the country from the forest of palms and curlicues to the simple lines of the late eighteenth century. The East Room was his greatest success in the White House. He had exact ideas concerning its décor: after three new chandeliers were installed in crystal and bronze, and hung with thousands of pendants, he had them taken down and disassembled to reduce them by six inches in diameter.

His final touch was to dispense with carpeting and to lay in a handsome parquet oak floor. Simplicity and elegance were restored—at least for the adults. But shortly after the new floor was finished, waxed and polished, an official looked into the East Room:

"One can imagine our surprise to see it covered with spiral lines of shallow but broad ruts. Upon inquiry we found that the Roosevelt children were the only ones near the room. When questioned, they replied: 'We thought it would make a fine roller skating rink and we found it dandy.' Mrs Roosevelt was informed and there was no more skating in the East Room."

72   Rather far removed from monarchial usage!

"When General Grant became President Grant, he put false, elaborate timbers across the ceiling and furnished the room in a style crossing ancient Greece with what someone called 'Mississippi River Boat.' The predominant feature became the three cut-glass chandeliers."

The columns and beams were ornamented with white and gilt woodwork. The new furniture was ebony and gold and the mantels were massive gold and white.

73

The East Room, March 4, 1889.
Benjamin Harrison's Inaugural Day. For festive occasions it was customary to decorate the columns with flowers worked into the design of the national shield.

74

"Under Presidents Arthur and McKinley, more and more potted palms were placed into the room until it looked like a jungle. This is the East Room just before Theodore Roosevelt ordered his changes."

The source of these plants was close at hand. The White House conservatories adjoined the East Room and visitors could stroll through an East Room door into the greenhouses.

75

"Theodore Roosevelt's renovation: the rug, the timbers, and most of the potted palms were discarded. The room is simple and classic. Theodore Roosevelt used it for his state functions and he once had a jujitsu exhibition there."

The architects made one basic change in Hoban's design. They removed the four great chimney breasts which projected two and a half feet into the room. The flues were set into the walls. (The chimneys can be seen in the earlier photograph of the East Room under Johnson.)

"There were no major changes in the East Room from 1902 to the present."

This is Mrs Kennedy's East Room. It is almost unchanged from President Truman's restoration. Some furniture has been removed and the fireplaces have been painted white.

A week before President Truman's election, it was found that the frescoed ceiling, weighing 70 pounds to the square foot, was sagging six inches. It was hastily propped up by scaffolding and the Trumans left the building.

President Truman replaced McKim's mantels with antique marble mantels of soft brown-red. Mrs Kennedy has now painted them and eventually plans to replace them with the same Georgian design that was used in the 1902 restoration. Except for the elimination of some Chippendale furniture which did not fit the room, Mrs Kennedy has done little to the East Room for reasons she now explains:

(*Mrs Kennedy and Mr Collingwood enter the East Room*)

MR COLLINGWOOD

Mrs Kennedy, this is the East Room pretty much as Americans have known it now for 60 years. Obviously you haven't felt that you had to make any great changes in it.

MRS KENNEDY

No, I think it's lovely. I hate to make changes really, so when you find a room like this, it's wonderful.

MR COLLINGWOOD

This piano brings to mind that this is the part of the White House where you have the musical affairs.

MRS KENNEDY

That's right. This piano, with eagle supports, was given to Franklin Roosevelt. And this is the end of the room where Pablo Casals played for us. We had a portable stage built when we had the Shakespeare Players.

MR COLLINGWOOD

Mrs Kennedy, this administration has shown a particular affinity for artists, musicians, writers, poets. Is this because you and your husband just feel that way or do you think that there's a relationship between the government and the arts?

MRS KENNEDY

That's so complicated. I don't know. I just think that everything in the White House should be the best—the entertainment that's given here and, if it's an American company that you can help, I like to do that. If it's not, just as long as it's the best.

MR COLLINGWOOD

Isn't that the famous Gilbert Stuart portrait of George Washington?

MRS KENNEDY

That's right. That's the oldest thing in the White House. The only thing that was here since the very beginning. A rather interesting precedent was set when that picture was painted. A commission was given to the finest living artist of the day to paint the President and later the government bought it for the White House. I often wish they'd followed that because so many pictures of later Presidents are by really inferior artists. There is another Gilbert Stuart portrait of Washington in the Cabinet Room. It was given by the Charles Paysons in memory of their son.

MR COLLINGWOOD

Is there anything else of great historical interest in this room?

MRS KENNEDY

There's more about this picture which is rather interesting. Gilbert Stuart painted the head from life and then the body was painted by people in his atelier which was a common practice in the eighteenth century and then Dolley Madison, when the White House was burned by the British in 1814, managed to save it.

79

After the White House was burned, Monroe came back in 1817 and had to refurnish it. So he bought all these superb bronzes in France. They're on the mantel now in the Green Room and the Blue Room. In the State Dining Room is perhaps the most famous of all, the Monroe centerpiece—masses and masses of gold and glass which were bought in France.

The First Floor

The Stuart portrait of Washington has generated one of the great legends of American folklore. For years American history books credited Dolley Madison with carving the portrait out of the frame with a kitchen knife as the British approached. The accurate story is more elaborate.

About 1796 the portrait was commissioned by Gardner Baker, who wanted it for a popular museum he owned in New York. Baker took it to Boston for exhibition. When he suddenly died of yellow fever it was sold to Andrew Laing who in July 1797 sold it for $800 to "the secretaries of the Department for the President's house." Thus Mrs Kennedy is accurate when she says it is the oldest object in the White House. When the rooms on the first floor were finished, the Stuart portrait was hung in the State Dining Room.

As the British approached Washington and President Madison left the White House to organize a defense force, Dolley Madison remained in the building gathering a wagonload of documents for safe keeping. They included a draft of the Declaration of Independence. America probably owes her a greater debt for saving these documents than for saving the portrait of Washington, but legend runs its own course.

She described her last moments in the White House in a letter to her sister:

"Will you believe it my sister? We had a battle or skirmish near Bladensburgh, and I am still here within the sound of cannon! . . . I insist on waiting until the large picture of George Washington is unscrewed from the wall. This process was found too tedious for these perilous moments; I ordered the frame to be broken and the canvas taken out.

"It is done and the precious portrait placed in the hands of two gentlemen from New York for safe keeping. On handing the canvas to the gentlemen in question, Messrs. Barker and De Peyster, Mr. Sioussat [her butler] cautioned them against rolling it up, saying that it would destroy the portrait." (Dolley had the name wrong: "Barker" should have been "Baker." She had the places wrong too: the gentlemen were not from New York but from New Orleans and Connecticut.)

80

Baker and De Peyster carried the portrait away in a cart, but became frightened and later abandoned it. A Negro boy, perhaps a slave, found the painting and took it to Georgetown. He left it at the Crawford Hotel. The hotel's owner was afraid of punishment if the British were to find him with a portrait of Washington. He placed the painting outdoors against a wall "exposed for three days to the clemency of the weather." Since contemporary observers remark that a hurricane put out the fire in the burning White House, the condition of a portrait left standing in a rainstorm can be imagined.

The Stuart painting was renovated at the time it was returned to the White House. The legend of Dolley's carving knife has never died, despite the fact that during later retouchings and reframings, no knife marks were found on the canvas. In 1848 Dolley wrote a letter to a New York newspaper, establishing what she knew of the gentlemen to whom she had entrusted the painting.

As the years passed, many people retouched and restored the canvas. What remained of Stuart's portrait disappeared under layers of paint. Stories circulated that it was executed by Winstanley or Stuart's daughter Jane—who would have been four years old at the time the British burned the White House!

A restoration in the 1930s re-established Gilbert Stuart as the painter. But some damage was permanent. The head is disproportionately large for the body, and the staring eyes are not in Stuart's style. The face shows his delicate brush strokes. The clothing and surroundings are certainly in the technique generally credited to him.

(*They cross the East Room and enter the Main Corridor*)

Some five tons of lighting equipment were brought into the White House for the taping. Mrs Kennedy used normal street makeup and did not require the services of a professional makeup artist.

The two boxes contain ficus; the flowers in the large urn are flowering quince, cymbidium orchids in shades of green, white stock, carnations, and chrysanthemums.

The Stuart portrait of Washington. The oversized head is apparent, even in this black-and-white photograph.

83

At the time of Mrs Kennedy's tour, the Monroe candelabras on the mantel of the East Room were still awaiting minor repairs so that the candles would stand straight in the holders. The pair of candelabras was ordered in France by President Monroe in 1817. He paid 1400 francs (about $275 at the time) for them. The vase is part of the Monroe bronze collection.

The Main Corridor and Hall

Exiting the East Room, Mrs Kennedy enters the main corridor.

Mrs Kennedy's tour was greatly simplified by the use of a small microphone and a transmitter, both of which were concealed under the jacket of her suit. Aerials were hidden behind draperies and doors to receive the weak transmissions from her battery-powered broadcasting set. These technical devices eliminated cables and booms, thus permitting Mrs Kennedy almost complete freedom to walk wherever she pleased.

This is the corridor which leads across the White House to the State Dining Room.

MRS KENNEDY

That's right. I rather love this hall. It has all the colors one thinks of when one thinks of the White House: red and white and blue and gold. It also has four of the best American pictures which have been loaned to us for the White House, including the only other Gilbert Stuart—of John Barry who founded the Navy.

All the heads of state come through this door. This is where the President meets them. Here is where the Marine Band plays, and they have ruffles and flourishes, and "Hail to the Chief." Then there's a receiving line and everyone goes into dinner in the State Dining Room.

(*They cross the hall to the State Dining Room*)

The main corridor has always had a remote, museumlike feeling. No one has ever been able to make it look warm. Many First Ladies have tried to soften this area of cold stone and columns by placing flowers and portraits throughout the hall. Hoban's original intention seems clear: a formal, un-adorned area which would announce the dignity of the house.

But the problems of esthetic warmth were nothing compared to the cold drafts that originated in this part of the house. As early as 1837 Martin Van Buren tried to screen it off. A clear glass partition was erected to keep the wind from entering the parlors. The problem of warmth could not be solved until the White House was equipped with central heating. Although President Grant had a boiler and a new heating system installed, he felt the need for a screen. Again, a glass wall was installed.

The center hall is best described in terms of traffic control. Guests move through it to receptions in any of the state parlors, and the White House ushers are stationed in the central hall to guide visitors to the room in which they are expected.

In an effort to heighten interest in the otherwise formal entrance hall and corridor, Mrs Kennedy has hung a number of significant portraits. This is Commodore John Barry, often called the Father of the Navy. It was painted by Gilbert Stuart, whose portrait of Washington hangs in the East Room. This Barry portrait is a far better example of the artist's work.

87

"This is the same entrance as it was in 1881 when President Arthur had it redone. This was before the time of central heating, and to keep the drafts out, Chester Arthur commissioned Louis Tiffany to build this elaborate glass screen."

Louis Tiffany was a close friend of Chester Arthur and the most famous decorator in New York. A cut-glass screen in high Victorian style and elaborate decorations worked into the ceiling and walls were an attempt at a solution. He described the motifs of interlaced eagles and flags as being in "the Arabian method," but the colored glass recalls the windows of the Tsars' apartments in the Kremlin. Visitors admired hidden doors which "magically" opened at various parts of the screen. Some other of Louis Tiffany's screens lasted until Franklin Roosevelt, but the center hall was cleared by Charles Follen McKim in 1902.

88

The main entrance hall shortly after the 1902 renovation by McKim, Mead & White. One of Theodore Roosevelt's first orders was to "break in small pieces that Tiffany screen." The portrait of Theodore Roosevelt is by John Singer Sargent and is one of the few good presidential portraits in the White House.

President Truman thought it inappropriate for the President's Seal to be placed on the floor of the hall, where visitors would walk across it. He ordered it removed.

The main reception hall of the main corridor.

The North Portico is on the other side of the door. Pennsylvania Avenue lies beyond. This door is rarely used, except for affairs of state. The outgoing President meets the incoming Chief Executive on either side of the door behind Mrs Kennedy. Chiefs of foreign states are also welcomed here when they arrive on official visits.

"This is the State Dining Room as it was during the time of President Grant and his wife, Julia. Originally, the State Dining Room would hold only fifty or sixty people."

In this crude, quickly done sketch, the artist has distorted the Monroe candelabra which Mrs Grant placed on the table. However, the chairs are accurately drawn. A few are still in the White House and have been placed in the Treaty Room on the second floor. Mrs Kennedy was able to date the chairs from sketches similar to this.

The same room, seventeen years later. In 1888 Grover Cleveland's guests sit on straight-back chairs. The artist is far more sophisticated, and the drawing of the men is a precursor of the style that Charles Dana Gibson would make famous.

92

The State Dining Room before Theodore Roosevelt made his changes. The straight-back chairs are the same as those in the preceding sketch. The mantel in the background will be seen in Mrs Kennedy's Red Room. The room is at its most fussy and elaborate. The contrast is marked between this photograph and the one immediately following.

"Just outside the State Dining Room there used to be a stairway leading to the upper floor. This staircase and hall were eliminated in 1902."

The staircase led to the family quarters on the west side of the second floor. It was eliminated to provide more space for the State Dining Room. This was the most important structural change made by the architects.

"The State Dining Room was simplified in 1902 . . . the capacity of the room was more than doubled. Theodore Roosevelt hung his stuffed animal heads around the room. There's a story that President Wilson so disliked these stuffed heads that he always seated himself in such a manner that he would not see them while eating."

Architecturally, the room is simpler. The animal heads, the large chairs, and the hangings are contradictory to the basic plan, but they are forgiveable because they represent Theodore Roosevelt's personal taste.

A detail of the mantel.

—This photograph is prophetic: Theodore Roosevelt was to splinter the Republican Party by organizing his "Bull Moose" faction. The photograph dates 1903. "Bull Moose" would appear as TR's standard in the 1912 election. President Wilson may have disliked these animal heads, but "Bull Moose" so split the Republicans that the Democrats and Wilson were elected.

—This mantel, showing carved buffalo heads, was replaced by a simple molding in 1952. Mrs Kennedy plans to install a copy similar to the one shown here.

The State Dining Room
. . . and tableware

The State Dining Room, rehearsal scene.

Although the room can seat 102 people, the table was set for only 30. The table remained set for three days during the production period. Flowers were changed daily.

MR COLLINGWOOD

This State Dining Room symbolizes your duties as an official hostess. Do you serve many meals here?

MRS KENNEDY

Yes, this is where all the State Dinners and Lunches are given. It can seat 102 people, though the table now is not set up for that many.

MR COLLINGWOOD

Are there many State Dinners?

MRS KENNEDY

Yes, there are. There were almost two a month last year.

The knives, forks and spoons are all gold or vermeil. Previous Presidents used Monroe's knives and forks but so many of them have been lost that they've been copied. And the china is the Eisenhower gold china. You see, so many of the beautiful old services the Presidents had were destroyed and broken that now the Truman and the Eisenhower china is all that there's enough left of to use. And there is the beautiful Monroe centerpiece and his flower or fruit baskets and candelabra all brought from France in 1817. And these glasses, they're ours—I wanted a very simple design so that the china and silver and glass would show up more so I looked all over and the prettiest ones I found came from West Virginia.

This tablecloth is new. It's a gift to the White House from the

The State Dining Room as it appears when the table is not set for dinner.

A detail of the Monroe plateau. Candles or small vases for flowers can be set in the crowns held by the extended arms. The flowers are an arrangement of red, white and shades of blue anemone, white tulips, paper white narcissus with stevia at the base.

The centerpiece or plateau is the most elaborate of the bronzes which Monroe ordered from France. It is composed of seven mirrored sections surrounded by a band ornamented with fruits and flowers. Sixteen figures of Bacchantes are placed around the plateau. When fully extended, the centerpiece is 13½ feet long and 2 feet wide. Its original cost was the equivalent of $1125.

99

If you are invited to a state dinner at the White House, this is the place setting. The Monroe centerpiece is in the background. The glasses are classic tulip shape. The matches read "The President's House." The napkin is gold embossed. The china is the Eisenhower pattern.

The knives, forks, and spoons are vermeil (gold fired into silver). The original pieces have long since disappeared, or have worn out. These are copies made as recently as 1952.

firm of Porthault and it's all embroidered in gold to match the centerpiece and the knives and forks.

MR COLLINGWOOD

There are three portraits in this room, two behind us.

MRS KENNEDY

Yes. These two are on loan from the Boston Museum of Fine Arts. There's Thomas Jefferson, a copy after Stuart. And then there's Daniel Webster who didn't live here but he visited the White House for 40 years. And then over the mantel is the most famous one of all—the one of Abraham Lincoln which traditionally always hung in the State Dining Room. All three pictures are by Healy. Healy was a contemporary of Lincoln but he only saw him once, so he painted this picture from photographs.

MR COLLINGWOOD

This is a perfectly beautiful room. Have you changed it a great deal?

MRS KENNEDY

No. We painted it white. This room's interesting because it has the most architectural unity of any room in the White House. It's really all 1902. It's interesting, people always think of Theodore Roosevelt with his stuffed animals and things. Few people realize that he was second only to Thomas Jefferson in his care and knowledge of the White House. In fact he designed the one thing which is missing here and which will soon be given to us —a superb mantel. McKim, Mead and White had designed one with lion's heads but Theodore Roosevelt said, "No, the lion's

101

not an American animal." So he designed it with Buffalo heads of white marble and McKim, Mead and White now is copying that for us, so you'll soon see it here to replace this just simple molding that was installed in 1952.

MR COLLINGWOOD

The First Floor Mrs Kennedy, on that fireplace just under the mantel there's an inscription which I found one of the most moving things in the White House.

MRS KENNEDY

Yes. That's from the very first letter that was ever written from the White House. It was written by John Adams, the first President to live here, to his wife Abigail when he'd only been here two days—on November 2, 1800. In it he says "I pray heaven to bestow the best of blessings on this house, and on all that shall hereafter inhabit it. May none but honest and wise men ever rule under this roof." It was Franklin Roosevelt who loved that prayer and had it put on the mantelpiece.

(*They exit State Dining Room*)

102

103

These portraits of Thomas Jefferson, Daniel Webster and Abraham Lincoln are in the State Dining Room. They are painted by the American artist, George P. A. Healy (1813–92). Healy studied in France. At twenty-six, his success was assured when King Louis Philippe agreed to sit for him. When Healy returned home he became one of the leading portraitists of his time.

I Pray Heaven to Bestow
The Best of Blessings on
THIS HOUSE
and on All that shall hereafter
Inhabit it. May none but Honest
and Wise Men ever rule under This Roof

Mrs Kennedy reading the inscription on the State Dining Room Mantel.

A Short Detour . . .

The Red Room in the 1860s.

Early Victorian pieces, except for the table which is Empire. To modern eyes, the room seems fussy, but (as the following pictorial essay shows) this Red Room would seem almost Spartan to later Victorians. The walls are relatively simple, and are in the Greek revival period that was fashionable at the time.

The small stools are something like the tabourets that prompted Congressman Ogle to liken the furnishings of the White House to the courts of Europe. All the furniture may be hand made. The strongest possibility is that this room was furnished by President Buchanan whose tastes ran heavily to Louis XV lines. The oval chairs are Victorian adaptations of Louis XV.

105

John Adams' hope for "good and honest men" to rule under the White House roof has political as well as sentimental overtones. Even the purely ceremonial events of the White House are scrutinized, discussed, divided and sub-divided in the hard game of American politics. Mrs Kennedy's line concerning glassware is a minor example: "I looked all over and the prettiest ones I found came from West Virginia." The politically oriented assumed that her reference was no accident, but part of the administration's policy of repaying a debt to West Virginia.

Those who see only politics recalled that West Virginia put John Kennedy in the forefront of the 1960 Democratic race. A Protestant, poverty stricken border state, West Virginia was the crucial test of John Kennedy who made specific pledges to relieve the state's unemployment problems. There is a glassware factory in West Virginia: ergo, after West Virginia gave him the Democratic primary the glassware showed up on the dining table, and, ergo, Mrs Kennedy mentioned the state by name. So runs the politician's argument. A few weeks after the White House tour was broadcast, part of another television program presided over by a distinguished commentator read this political analysis into Mrs Kennedy's remarks.

This is not the place to dissect this analysis of Mrs Kennedy's motives. These glasses *are* pretty, and always have been pretty—ever since the wine growers of France invented the tulip shape. Our burden is that John Adams' hope refers as much to politics as to statesmanship. Every President is a politician who must pick his way through promises, pledges, platforms, and pressures. Most have used the welfare of the nation as their primary guide through the thicket. Adams' hope has been answered.

Yet, in passing through the political hedgerows, some Presidents have been badly scratched. The lovely Monroe centerpiece and the gold spoons on the table wounded one President. The centerpiece defeated Martin Van Buren's plans for re-election, and changed the décor of the White House forever. For these reasons, a detour in our annotations seems in order.

Mrs Kennedy has already told part of the story. James Monroe had the great task of furnishing the White House after the burning. One solution was to bring his personal property into the building. A government estimator surveyed his pieces and valued them at $9071.22½. He billed the government. At the same time he ordered furniture and bronze and silver pieces from France. Monroe's furniture will be discussed later—but the centerpiece (or *surtout de table*) has remained in the White House ever since.

James Monroe's purchase of bric-a-brac alarmed a few Congressmen. The 13-foot centerpiece cost some 6000 francs (or $1125.00 at the time) and hardly seemed in keeping with republican simplicity. The protest was not very strong; the pieces were handsome and obviously a good bargain—the manufacturer complained that he "lost by it nearly 2000 francs." The bronze and silver pieces stayed in the White House through the administrations of John Quincy Adams and Andrew Jackson. President Jackson spent $50,000 for additional furniture, a great deal of which was imported from Europe. Though Congress had appropriated the money, the bills were not all paid until Martin Van Buren took office. President Van Buren had more modest needs than Andrew Jackson. On April 14, 1840—some 33 years after Monroe had ordered the centerpiece—a bill was presented to Congress for $3665. The money was to pay for repairing furniture, and buying trees and manure for landscaping the White House. President Van Buren had sent Monroe's silver centerpiece out for gilding. Congressman John Ogle of Pennsylvania got up to speak.

Van Buren was a Democrat as was Jackson. Ogle was a Whig, and the Whigs had been in political eclipse. Originally, they had been the party of the eastern aristocratic and financial interests and had gone down to defeat before the Democrats and Andrew Jackson. Out of power for twelve years, the Whigs regrouped around frontier folklore. They became the "log cabin party." Their candidate, William Henry Harrison, was presented as a hard-fisted son of toil who lived in a log cabin. (In fact, Harrison was a cultured gentleman from Virginia and the timbers of his spacious Ohio home had been finished by more than an ax.) There had been a depression in 1837; the frontier states had greatly increased their voting power; Van Buren had not caught the popular imagination—and the Whigs saw their chance. What better way to attack than to show that the White House was luxuriating in monarchial splendor while the country suffered? The Whigs meant to demonstrate that Van Buren was removed from the common people, and did not understand their problems. The State Dining Room was the center of Congressman Ogle's attack. He refrained from emphasizing that it was the Whig, Monroe, who had spent $1125.00 for the centerpiece. It was the Democrat, Van Buren, who had it gilded at a cost of $75.00.

Congressman Ogle rose to deliver his speech. It was called "The Regal Splendor of the President's Palace," later known as the "Gold Spoon Speech." Too long and stylistically dated for current tastes, it is still a masterpiece of nascent proletarian literature. (Our punctuation is taken from Ogle's published speech.) Ogle was out to get Van Buren—beginning with the salary of the President.

The Congressman reported that the President's salary worked out to "$68.50 per day or $2.81 *for each and every hour*."

"I can inform you, sir; he has not only taken *twenty five thousand dollars*

107

in gold and silver for his annual salary but he has compelled the people to pay for HEMMING HIS OWN DISH RAGS into the bargain."

And what was Van Buren truly after?

"It will not be very inconvenient for *President* Van Buren to exchange his splendid Spanish cloak for a royal stole and having placed the crown upon his head, the diadem on his brow, and bedecked his person with the royal jewels, with the laquered sceptre in his hand, take his seat on that throne. And thus this democratic *President,* although deprived of the *title* of royalty will be invested, not only with its *perogatives,* but with its *trappings,* also."

Congressman Ogle knew the secret signs by which one member of the royalty makes himself known to another, though both may be in simple, republican clothes. The tabouret (a stool, with neither arms nor back) is the clandestine sign of incipient monarchy. Van Buren had spent $8.00 to recover four tabourets.

"Even before the Crusades THE HONORS OF THE TABOURET were held in highest esteem. By ceremonial law in many monarchies no individual in the kingdom is entitled to enjoy this high distinction save a DUTCHESS OF THE BLOOD ROYAL."

The monarchial plot was sinister enough. Worse, of course, were the expenditures. Van Buren had repapered the whole East Room, at a cost of $346.00 for paper and labor. Jackson had bought a few dozen chairs and benches for the same room at a cost of $600.00. Ogle was attacking both Presidents.

"Ay, Sir, every plain republican will now find a set of chairs in that splendid and royal saloon, which took the round sum of six hundred dollars of the PEOPLE'S CASH to pay for. Is that not 'sitting down' with a vengeance?"

Room by room, page by page, John Ogle made an inventory of the White House. The White House glittered with splendor. And what would the people say to these Frenchy ways and regal accommodations? What would "the Hoosiers, Buckeyes and Wolverines say of the Blue Room?—in which Van Buren receives his sleek and ribband-bedecked courtiers, as they present themselves with their humblest genuflexions and prostrations, crouching like fawning spaniels to the hand which has it in its power to throw them a bone?"

But the core of contempt is the State Dining Room. Food and utensils are universal. Extravagance in the dining room is easily understood.

"I must inform you that this table is not provided with those old and unfashionable dishes, 'hog and hominy,' 'fried meat and gravy' with a mug of hard cider." No, "there is no food for the palate placed on this table. There is a feast of gold for the eyes that would have satiated King Midas himself.

"Oh! Sir, how delightful it must be to a real genuine locofoco [Democrat] to eat his *paté de foie gras, dinde desossé* and *salade à la volaile* from a SILVER PLATE with a GOLDEN KNIFE AND FORK. And how exquisite to sip with a GOLDEN SPOON his *soupe à la Reine* from a SILVER TUREEN. It almost 'makes my mouth water' to talk about it."

Centered in the speech is the Monroe plateau. "It does appear to me, Sir, that the Plateau, with its fine *mirrors* in which the honest Democrats can look at themselves almost every minute during the formal progress of a court banquet would be regarded even by a Bank whig as a pretty formidable article of furniture."

Ogle goes on to list a seven-course dinner accompanied by eight wines— all dishes listed in French. After dinner, he references Fanny Kemble, an English actress with whom Van Buren was acquainted:

"What sir will the honest locofocos say to Mr. Van Buren for spending the people's cash in FOREIGN FANNY KEMBLE GREEN FINGER CUPS, in which to wash his pretty tapering, soft, white, lily fingers, after dining on fricandeau de veau and omelette souffle?"

Ogle's speech was not an unimportant fact in the defeat of Martin Van Buren. One year later, when the Whig John Tyler was President, the newspapers were calling the White House "the public shabby house." The description was far more accurate than Ogle's.

It has been remarked that Ogle's speech changed the décor of the White House forever. For the next sixteen years only small amounts of money were spent on the building. Presidents were cautious—not only because of Ogle— but because the leading political influences came from the frontier.

This detour from Mrs Kennedy's remarks is an illustration of the political considerations that play a part in the choice of objects for the house. Anyone who has watched his furniture being moved into a new house under the eyes of new neighbors has some understanding of the feelings of a First Lady when she changes the White House. Details which are insignificant in any other refurnishing can become affairs of state in the President's house.

The major themes in refurnishing have already been stated: First Families often look on the White House as a hotel; Congress uses appropriations as a lever for and against the President; and the over-all plan has usually been to call someone in and have him make the White House look up-to-date. All these are conscious and predictable themes; yet below the surface there are even stronger movements which are harder to define. The White House responds to the *taste* of America, as well as to its politics. America's taste in furnishings responds to the history of our country.

Democracy, to state it frankly, has made a shambles of furniture design. If the White House furnishings are seen in a vacuum, one yearns for the simplicity of the French Monarchy. During 150 years the tastes of three Louis' ruled Continental furnishings. In 160 years the White House has seen thirty-four Presidents and every style from the Bourbons to borax. Shortly after the maturing of American democracy came the rise of machine tooling and the fall of hand-carved furniture. A great struggle between hand workers and machine workers culminated in the Victorian.

If the reader will permit Mrs Kennedy to wait in the State Dining Room, this detour which started in politics will now wander through the greatest influence in White House furnishings: the Victorian.

In Congressman Ogle's day hand-carved furniture was still being made. So long as there was no competition from machines, the lines were simple. But as the factory replaced individual artisans, jigs, lathes, and gouges copied the simple designs at a lower price. In desperation the cabinetmakers began to carve more elaborate pieces, thus hoping to keep their lead over the machines. As the machines were perfected, the factory could duplicate anything the hand workers invented. Individual artisans tightened the spiral with even more rococo designs: the chief carver at the factory closed the gap and moved ahead. It was a deadly race to embellish the embellishments. By 1850 the Victorian seized the White House.

There were no alternatives. France, which had supplied decorative inspiration for two hundred years, was repetitive and sterile. Both England and France faced the same dilemma of man versus machine.

The Victorian was not one style, or one series of lines. Nor was it solely English. Cross influences of German, French, and Spanish invaded the furniture. Every ancient culture, and every new one (including Turkish nook with ottoman and red harem lamp) was seized upon. Each furniture factory had its own stylist and their chief carvers swallowed China and Egypt whole. In its later days Victorian was simply called "The Indescribable" or "The Reign of Terror." Paris and Baltimore had given way to Grand Rapids. The furniture became so heavy that casters were placed under chairs; otherwise the pieces could not have been moved. Every wood was used, although the period is sometimes called "Black Walnut and Horsehair."

The sight of wood itself became as shocking to the gentler Victorians as a lady's calf shown in public. First the wood was tasseled, then fringed, and finally covered and tufted. The framework totally disappeared.

Not all the pieces were bad. Both factories and cabinetmakers made a

110

few striking designs which are becoming appreciated today. But democracy had raised the living standards of millions of Americans who wanted the newest and the best—and plushness and ornateness were the obvious signs by which the newly rich advertised themselves. The climax of Victorian design was reached in the Mauve Decade—the 1890s.

In the same period the White House had been described by an extraordinarily competent reporter, Frank Carpenter. He attended one of President Cleveland's receptions:

". . . a thousand bare backs and bare necks gleamed under the gaslight of the East Room's magnificent chandeliers. A thousand men were in danger of colds in their claw hammer coats and the archdemon Pneumonia had plenty of chance to pick out his victims. At least 400 women were wearing diamonds of various sizes. I counted 50 pairs of solitaire earrings whose stones were as big as the end of my thumb and 3 diamond stars and pendants, any one of which would buy a large farm."

Yet the opulence did not overcome the shabbiness of the building. Carpenter saw it clearly:

". . . amid all its magnificence there are many bits of the commonplace and in spots it is actually shabby. As we came up through the handsome porte-cochere, we looked over the iron railing and saw the President's servants ironing his nightshirts and other unmentionable garments in the basement. The varnish is cracked upon the grained woodwork, and beside the door leading to the second story is a walnut umbrella stand that would be dear at five dollars. The door and stairs that brought us to the President's offices are covered with an old piece of Brussels carpet which was good once, but which has been patched, sewed, and resewed. It would not bring 50 cents at an auction. Against the wall in the upper hall stand a couple of 3 dollar wicker chairs and over the desk hangs a calendar bearing the advertisement of a railroad."

Victorian curlicues and geegaws were particularly out of place in the rooms of the White House. The balance and proportion of Hoban's simple rooms were lost, not only by the heavily ornamented furnishings, but by the rage for flowers. The greenhouses adjacent to the White House had grown to an enormous size, and the art of floral decoration was as complicated as the state of the furniture. Mrs Benjamin Harrison was a floriculturist who wreathed the banquet table in the State Dining Room with flowers.

President Arthur's table decorations included an arrangement "in the style of the Hanging Gardens of Babylon."

The history of furniture has always been one of action and reaction. It was obvious that the floridity would be succeeded by austerity, but austerity

111

had previously been prompted by great social changes—like revolutions or military conquests. Turn-of-the-century America had Spartan elements in it, but they were not about to take over power.

The American reaction to Victorian came from the American social scene. The architects had invented a new form: the skyscraper. The Chicago school of architects—particularly Louis Sullivan—found that Victorian and Greek lines were inapplicable to the problems presented by the skyscraper. In 1890 Sullivan designed the Wainwright Building in St. Louis. It was a clear trumpet announcing a new style, but it would take America a few decades to understand the new simplicity of Sullivan and his student, Frank Lloyd Wright. It would take even longer to see the means by which the lines of a skyscraper could be applied to interior furnishings.

In 1893, again in Chicago, the Columbian Exposition was a plea by our finest architects to return to classicism. The Centennial Exposition of 1876 in Philadelphia had presaged the same message. If there was no new design, and if the Victorian was obviously sterile, why not return to the classic periods which had been defaced?

The style was called "neo-classic" and it entered the White House in 1902. The plan was to furnish the White House with pieces that were in style when the building was erected, thus bringing the walls and furniture into harmony. In particular, the 1902 restoration seized on a French style of 1802—the Directoire. For a short period, between King and Napoleon, France had invented a clear line that was destined to be timeless.

Not all traces of the Victorian were swept out of the White House. As in millions of other American homes, remnants of the old, tortured style remained. The old Victorian pieces were placed in lesser rooms, and disappeared gradually in the first twenty years of the twentieth century. To the extent that other American homes contained reproductions, the rule was still being followed that the White House is always furnished in modern. But in many ways it was a casuistic, uneasy solution.

However classic the French line of 1802 might be, it was inappropriate for a house which stood at the center of American history. Whatever the vulgarity of the American Victorian might have been, the pieces were real, not reproductions. The difference between a real Directoire chair and a close reproduction do not mean much except to a scholar of antiques—and except in the White House.

At the time the argument was logical, but esoteric. America was not ready to listen. The neo-classic period had to run its course. During the first half of the twentieth century, Presidents would move through America's most famous house, but the chairs they sat on, and the tables they used were copied

The First Floor

112

reflections of French and English lines dating from the last half of the eighteenth century and the first decade of the nineteenth century.

No one can fix the date when America found its history a necessity. The movement began in the White House in the 1920s, with Mrs Coolidge and Mrs Hoover. As World War II thrust America into world leadership, our history became more than a chronology to be memorized. Our past became a source of strength to be questioned and examined. As we were challenged by other powers it became necessary for us to discover whether our strength came from the wealth of a new continent, or whether the history of America would show that our power flowed from the basic system of representative government. We looked at our past—not from curiosity, but from necessity.

The First Floor

We found not only the philosophy of government, but more mundane things: chairs, sofas, desks, tables. They were American, they were well designed, and they answered the questions of décor in America's most historic house. The difference between a reproduction and an antique was no longer esoteric. With careful scholarship, enough money and enough time, two rooms of the White House have been furnished in genuine pieces of early American styles: the Green Room is early Federal, and the Red Room is American Empire.

113

The Green Room after the Civil War.

114   The woodworking exemplified by the backs of the chairs is becoming more
tortured. The competition between man and machine is leading to elaboration. On
the walls, the over-all pattern is an ominous note. Things are going to get worse.

The Green Room before 1890.

The small patterns are everywhere: carpet, walls, and chair fabrics. The furniture is machine-made Victorian, cut by a jigsaw in small pieces and either nailed or glued together. The screen before the fireplace will reappear later. There's a harem arrangement in the pillows before the mirror. The eye has no place to rest.

115

The Green Room, just after 1890.

   The central chairs are overstuffed Victorian, in a style sometimes called Pullman. There's a bent-wood parlor chair in the right foreground which contrasts strangely with the ornateness of the rest of the furniture. The harem pillows have been pushed next to the right wall, but the exotic is not overlooked—on the left side of the room is a screen in Chinese style. The lamp on the table is draped in silk and decorated with artificial flowers. Between this picture and the previous one, the convolutions of bare wood have been covered, tasseled and tufted—as if wood itself were too crude a material for eminent Victorians.

116

The Green Room about 1893.

   The era of plush and electricity has arrived. The over-all patterns have disappeared, and the Victorian woodwork is sunk deep in upholstery. The curious center
chair is a tête-à-tête for three people who wish to converse. There is a temporary
relief from fussiness.

117

The Green Room, about 1898.

The tête-à-tête is now covered in elaborate brocade. The patterns in the upholstery and in the new carpet hint that ornateness is about to return. The potted plants and the fringes continue the pressure of the Victorian. The whole style is drifting aimlessly. Americans of taste were sick of it, but had nowhere to turn. There was nothing in sight but more curlicues, patterns, and gee-gaws. Theodore Roosevelt and Charles Follen McKim thus turned to the past to find simplicity.

118

The Green Room in 1903.

Almost all traces of the Victorian have been removed. Except for the center table and Chinese urns flanking the mantel, the Victorian has been removed. A new crystal chandelier has been hung. The rug has been removed and the parquet floor is exposed. (Theodore Roosevelt's white bearskin rug was a personal eccentricity which disappeared shortly after the picture was taken.) The chairs show the influence of California. They are caned, and somewhat reminiscent of the Mission and Morris styles. The room has been changed greatly, but it is not yet finished.

119

The Green Room in 1904.

    Except for the portraits of the Presidents, the Green Room is more French than American. The chairs are imitation Directoire; the center table is Empire, and small details reflect France at the beginning of the nineteenth century. The screen before the fireplace is the only remaining Victorian artifact. The vulgarity of the Victorian is gone, replaced by imitations of French furnishings. The only link between décor and the White House is that the French styles are taken from the same date as the construction of the White House.

120

Store Room in the Garret.

7. Pair of best brass andirons.
32. Brass Carpet rods. 1. pair Iron Dogs.

Store Room no. 2.

1. Plateau in five parts with a set of ornaments.
5. Brass lamps. 2. vase lamps. 1. Cabeen lamp
3. Glass sconces out of order
1. Mahogany Table & large clothes Basket.
12. pillars & 2. childrens Mattresses. 2. Bolsters
2. large fire fenders. 2. pair large Brass andirons
1. large Brussels carpet
8. Cotton blankets
2. Old arm Chairs
1. Mahogany Table & remnant of Brussels carpet.

North West Corner — Lady's Dressing room.

4. night Tables and 8. Mahogany Chairs
a small bundle of Old Curtains.

Large Room — North Side.

1. elegant bedstead with white dimity curtains, bed,
  mattress, Counterpane & bolster
2. Chintz window Curtains
1. Sofa 12. fashionable Chairs, crimson and Gold
2. Mahogany Tables. 1. wash stand. 1 looking Glass.
1 elegant Lady's Dressing Table 1. toilet with trimmings
Brussels carpet on the floor — 1 stool to ascend the Bed.

Presidents Dressing Room

11. Chairs Crimson and Gold
3. Suits dimity window Curtains with cornices
1. Bidet and a mahogany Table. common Carpet on
  floor.

33059

A part of the earliest inventory of White House furnishings—written by Thomas Jefferson in the same elegant script in which he drafted the Declaration of Independence.

Red Parlor

Date	Vo.	Description		
Aug. 6	19	For 77 5/8 yds. silk damask	621 00	
10	20	" furniture fringe, tassel fringe, tassel drapery edging	193 00	
		" 3 pieces of scroll furniture	9 00	
		" 6 " " gimp "	18 00	
		" 2 pr. curtain loops "	20 00	
		" 75 yds. silk lining for draperies	75 00	
		" 15 " interlining " "	11 75	
		" regilding in gold 12 pieces of furniture	152 00	
		" set of brass casters for chair	1 50	
		" upholstering & repairing 12 pcs. of furniture	96 00	1,196 75
Sept. 13	22	For 2 large best Holland shades	11 52	
21	24	" 20 yds. of wilton velvet carpet @ $4.00	80 00	
28	55	" laying 109 1/3 yds. of carpet	6 56	
		" laying matting	15 40	
		" taking up old matting	4 40	
		" 2 pr. silk window draperies 50/ 1 bookcase portier 150	51 50	
		" table covers 5.00 3 wall cabinet covers 6.00 brass screen 2.50	13 00	
		" cover for back of gold screen	1 75	
		" 88 yds. of matting laid	35 20	219 33
Oct. 26	56	For altering & refinishing 2 stands	2 00	2 00
Nov. 29	57	For 1 shade cord	20	
26	20	" 1 high back antique arm chair	19 50	19 70
Dec. 1	1	For furnishing materials & covering sofa & armchair in leather	64 85	
		" 2 best Holland shades (green) @ 3.84	7 68	72 53
1902				
Jany. 23	46	For 1 Khorason Rug	145 00	
	49	" 1 Rocker 18.00 1 Durham sofa 45.00	63 00	208 00
Feby. 3	12	For 1 4-fold black screen	4 00	4 00
Mch. 15	8	For furnishing material & putting up brass travis pole	2 30	
		" burnishing brass pole 1.50 for 1 pr. pulls 50	2 00	
		" 1 bank cord 30/ for 1 1/2 doz. travis rings 3.00	3 30	
22	30	" repairing French clock	2 50	10 10
Apl. 5	6	For 1 shade cord	25	25
May 3	8	For 1 new tin roller for repairing shade	90	90

A page from a White House accounts book during the change of administrations from McKinley to Roosevelt.

The Red Room
. . . and American Empire

Outside the Red Room stands the pier table which Joseph Bonaparte brought to the United States. It is pure French Empire. The Egyptian-Greek head carved at the top of the leg is a caryatid; a design which had been introduced at the end of the eighteenth century. The relationship between this leg and the mantel in a forthcoming Red Room photograph is mentioned by Mrs Kennedy.

The portrait is that of the Revolutionary general, John Stark. It was painted by Samuel F. B. Morse, who invented the telegraph.

Pier tables almost always have mirrors between the back legs. The function of the mirror is demonstrated by the photograph: it was used by ladies to verify their skirts and trains.

The glass of water next to the flower basket was at hand throughout the taping. Mrs Kennedy drank water to keep her throat clear and to prevent dehydration under heavy lighting.

123

Next to the State Dining Room is the Red Room. It is generally agreed that the Red Room has been one of the great successes of the current restoration. During the television broadcast Mrs Kennedy entered the Red Room from the corridor which connects to the State Dining Room and she stopped by a pier table for the following remarks:

The First Floor

(*They enter corridor*)

MR COLLINGWOOD

Mrs Kennedy, I know that after a dinner in the State Dining Room it's customary to withdraw to the Red Room. May we?

MRS KENNEDY

Yes, it's right here. It's one of the rooms that's used the most, so I'd like to show you what we've done to it. But before we go to the Red Room you should look at this pier table; it's Empire and it belonged to Joseph Bonaparte, Napoleon's brother, who came here after Waterloo.

He lived in Bordentown, New Jersey, and had lots of his beautiful furniture with him. And his furniture was very important in transferring the French Empire style to America. This is lent to us by the Philadelphia Museum.

(*They exit corridor*)

When Congressman Ogle attacked President Van Buren for using the furniture of kings, ordinary people were using ordinary furniture—which had been designed for an emperor. Empire furniture held center stage in

124

America from the late 1830s through the 1850s. American Empire (sometimes called late Federal) derives directly from Bonaparte, the Corsican who ruled France from 1803 through 1812. Its style and history are intimately related to the American scene, but some French background is necessary.

Napoleon advertised himself with his furniture. He was a military dictator and an emperor; not a king. The gilded woods of Bourbon monarchs were not for him. He stripped the paint and gold from the wood and announced his strength in dark mahogany and hard angles and curves. The somber wood was a perfect background on which to hang bronze ornaments, and the emperor advertised himself with bronze trademarks. The bee, the lion, the gorgon, the sphinx: all had specific meanings, recalling Emperor Bonaparte's consulship, conquests, and coronation. The Empress Josephine chose the swan as her emblem. The furniture was not intended to be comfortable. A French writer said: "Precautions are needed to avoid being bruised by the most gentle use of your furniture."

Why should this brassy, French furniture become a leading style in America?

For many reasons: in the first decade of the 1800s America was violently anti-British, and strongly pro-French. Our Revolution was followed by the French Revolution and sympathy caromed across the Atlantic. Emissaries and ministers moved between the countries. French immigration to America has never been substantial but the opening of the nineteenth century was an exceptional era. Refugees from the Revolution and the counterrevolution fled to America. Some of the best cabinetmakers of Paris arrived in New York, Rhode Island, and Maryland. American-French relationships were at their best.

Another factor, far less intellectual, was that the French Empire line appealed to the rising merchant class of America. Early Federal was delicate, rational, and quiet; it was deliberately unostentatious and cool. A new class of solid citizens wanted solid furniture. American Empire was thicker and thus more impressive than the early Federal pieces. Federal furniture had no bronzework, but the gleam of Empire bronze mountings and figures was an obvious sign of wealth. Empire showed pomp without circumstance and richness without royalty.

A final reason was economic. Competition had begun for the expanding American market. Federal furniture required careful cabinetmaking: Empire was easier to carve. Any cabinetmaker with a little skill could turn it out. Machinery for making furniture was introduced about 1820, and the massive, uncomplicated lines of Empire were easily adaptable to the first crude jigs. The battle between cabinetmaker and machine was announced

125

—the triumph of the machine would not take place until the Victorian era.

As American taste turned toward Empire, the master cabinetmakers of the Federal period tried to follow the trend. The pieces of Mrs Kennedy's Red Room reflect the counterattack of these handiworkers.

Though there is no Duncan Phyfe in the room, his story is typical. Phyfe was born in Scotland, apprenticed in Albany and had his workshops in New York. The prophet of the Federal period tried to meet the competition. He bought only the best materials. Exporters from Santo Domingo and Cuba would refer to their choicest pieces of timber as "Duncan Phyfe logs." Sometimes he would pay as much as a thousand dollars for a single log, and the glue used was the best Peter Cooper could supply. Some fine examples of Duncan Phyfe's best period are on display in the ground floor Library—a room which was not complete at the time of Mrs Kennedy's tour.

Unfortunately, Phyfe could not hold against the competition. In his later years he turned out cruder but more salable pieces which he bitterly called "butcher furniture." In 1847 Duncan Phyfe withdrew, beaten. He closed the door of his Fulton Street shop and spent the balance of his life making small objects for his family.

America did not swallow French Empire whole. For example, the Napoleonic gilt symbols were modified. The American eagle and star were obvious substitutions for the more blatant signs of the emperor. Mahogany gave way to native woods, particularly from forests of the Midwest. A simpler style, Biedermeier, was a German adaptation of French Empire, and it followed the German wave of immigration into Michigan, Wisconsin, and Illinois. Brass and gilded ornamentation disappeared from less expensive furnishings. Finally, although America might be in revolt against British ideas, the traditions of Sheraton and Adam were not totally discarded. The United States began its Empire period under a heavy French influence, but American Empire became a style to itself. Its later styles slipped into the Victorian: a writer noted "Never have the worlds of the fashionable and the beautiful been further apart."

At best, Empire furniture in an Empire setting is as brilliant as a brass choir of bugles. The Red Room of the White House is the only room which Mrs Kennedy has done over completely. It has a flash of fire unduplicated throughout the building. Yet it is a parlor; still comfortable.

The First Floor

126

(They enter the Red Room)

MRS KENNEDY

Everything in this room is Empire, because the style of the room is dictated by the mantelpiece which is Empire. This is one of the only two remaining mantels in the White House from 1817 after the fire. All the ones before were burned and all others in the house are either 1902 or '48.

MR COLLINGWOOD

Which of these pieces have historical associations?

MRS KENNEDY

Oh, there's quite a few. This is Dolley Madison's sofa. That's Nellie Custis' sofa, Martha Washington's granddaughter. The most interesting are the pair of chairs by the desk. They date from before Van Buren or Tyler. These chairs were a gift of Mrs Edythe McGinnis of Falls Church, Virginia. So we're very lucky and grateful.

MR COLLINGWOOD

What is the fabric?

MRS KENNEDY

It's silk with a scroll border of gold. It's copied from an American Empire document.

MR COLLINGWOOD

I know that all of the rooms in the White House have historical associations but this room, next to the State Dining Room, must   127

The Red Room as Mrs Kennedy has furnished it. The Red Room is the only room which she has completely redecorated. This is one of a pair of mantels originally in the State Dining Room. It was moved in 1902.

128

have been used so often a great many things must have happened here.

MRS KENNEDY

Yes, one thing that's interesting: President Hayes was sworn in here as President secretly at night 'cause his was the closest election there ever was and they didn't want the United States to be without a President for even a day so while everyone was having dinner, they swore him in here.

MR COLLINGWOOD

These pictures are good too. That one behind you is a Civil War picture. Has that been here in the White House long?

MRS KENNEDY

No, that's the picture that my committee to get pictures for the White House found for here. It's wonderful. It has such historic interest. "Civil War Maneuvers" by Wordsworth Thompson. It depicts the action at Edwards Ferry and Balls Bluff, Virginia, in October 1861 when the commanding officer, Colonel E. D. Baker, was killed.

I feel so strongly that the White House should have as fine a collection of American pictures as possible. It's so important, the setting in which the presidency is presented to the world, to foreign visitors. And American people should be proud of it. We had such a great civilization, yet so many foreigners don't realize it. This little table, for instance; it's by Lannuier, a French cabinetmaker who came to America. Not many people know of him. But he was just as good as Duncan Phyfe or as the great French cabinetmakers. All the things we did so well, pictures, furniture —I think that this house should be the place where you can see them best.

129

The east side of the Red Room.

The sofa belonged to Dolley Madison. The painting shows the Civil War battle at Balls Bluff, Virginia. The chairs are American Empire.

The scrollwork on the wall fabric matches the design of the upholstered sofa and chairs. It is derivative of the Pompeiian decorations which so strongly influenced the French Empire period.

The round table is also influenced by Pompeii. Its top is inlaid marble, a common Roman motif. This Lannuier table is one of the few pieces in the White House which is of mint, museum value—aside from its inherent historic interest.

130

The Red Room is the most brilliant salon in the White House. The walls are fuchsia, and the bronze ornaments contrast with the dark wood of the furniture.

The northwest corner of the Red Room.

The sofa belonged to Nellie Custis, George Washington's granddaughter. Martha Washington was first married to Colonel Daniel Custis who died in 1757. When George Washington married her two years later, he legally adopted all her children. This sofa is pure American Empire. Its curved armrests and legs are a variation which Duncan Phyfe used. Much Empire furniture made heavy use of veneering— a process in which fine woods were sliced and placed atop simpler woods in a manner predating plywood. Hand veneered woods were cut in thicker slices, but one of the difficulties in finding good antiques is that modern central heating and rapid temperature changes cause the veneer to buckle and split.

131

The music stand in the background is in its customary position. It was moved across the room for the television program so that Mrs Kennedy might comment on it as she moved to the Blue Room.

MR COLLINGWOOD

And that's what your committee is doing?

MRS KENNEDY

The First Floor

They're trying to do. By the way, this is interesting. It's "Lafayette's March" composed and printed in 1824. He came here on a triumphal tour when he was an old man. The whole country went wild about him, wrote poems, made up songs, this is one of them. It's the same period as the room so we put it there.

(*They exit the Red Room*)

One of the strongest influences in the Red Room traces back to Pompeii. The scrollwork in the fabric reflects the Roman habit of ornamenting all large surfaces. The round Lannuier table is extraordinarily similar to Pompeiian tables, including the mosaic marble design.

To those who would follow the genealogy of style, a deep breath is cautioned before listing the derivations of style in the Red Room. The line started with the Greeks, who were copied by the Romans. (This can be seen in the female figures who support the mantel: they are Greek with a Roman influence.) The Romans were copied nineteen centuries later by the British and French. Napoleon salted the mixture with a heavy touch of Egyptian. The Americans borrowed from the borrowers and added a few touches of their own. Then the Americans split off—one group heading toward the Victorian and the other losing itself in the wilds of a second Greek revival.

The point is that furniture evolves, and is not invented, like the light bulb or telegraph key. Styles slip, slide, perish, decay—and are revived to fall again. Mrs Kennedy called the room "Empire," and one of her advisors was heard to mutter, "I wish she'd call it late Federal. In American furniture circles *nobody* buys Empire."

Other objects in the room are noteworthy. There is an imported French Empire desk between the windows which is equipped with secret drawers. This was a common practice until the art of safemaking had been perfected.

The sofa which belonged to Nellie Custis may bring some balm to those who want to know what is American in American Empire. The curved lines of the legs and armpieces are uniquely American—so is the shape of the object. The whole piece is so American that if one were to call it Empire before a French furniture dealer, he would probably smile as paternalistically as a French wine dealer who had just had his first sip of New York champagne.

The room has traditionally been one in which presidential portraits have been hung. For a time it was known as the Washington Room because the Gilbert Stuart portrait of George Washington hung here. Until recently the portrait of Grace Coolidge was in this room, but the fuchsia overtone in the new silk fabric clashed with the scarlet-red of Mrs Coolidge's velvet gown and the portrait has been moved to the China Room.

The painting, "Civil War Maneuvers" by Wordsworth Thompson, deserves further annotation. Colonel E. D. Baker, one of the leading officers in the Battle of Balls Bluff, was a close friend of the Lincoln family. The Lincolns had named their son, Tad, for him. The day before the battle Colonel Baker visited the Lincolns. The scene was noted by a passing officer who described Lincoln seated on the south lawn with his back against a tree, while Willie Lincoln played nearby. The colonel was stretched out prone on the grass, engrossed in an unrecorded conversation with the President. At the end of the interview Colonel Baker kissed Willie, mounted his horse, and rode away. He was killed the next day during the action depicted by the painting.

President Lincoln "left Headquarters, unheeding the salute of the orderly, both hands pressed to his heart, his features utterly convulsed with grief."

The south side of the Red Room.

The desk is French Empire. Almost everything else is American Empire. The desk contains secret drawers—a common practice until the art of safemaking had been perfected. Both tables were made by Charles Honoré Lannuier, a French cabinetmaker who immigrated to the United States. The rectangular table to the right shows a bird-woman in the style of winged victory; a theme that often recurs in Empire.

The brilliance of Empire furniture comes from the contrast between brass and dark wood. The Empire period reacted against the use of marquetry, and there are almost no examples of inlaid woods in the house.

134

A closer view of the two chairs donated by Mrs McGinnis. (A fuller explanation of these chairs will be found in the text annotating Mrs Kennedy's remarks in the Lincoln Room.)

The cables are light and camera lines. The television technicians worked cautiously and left the White House without breaking or marring a single object.

United States Department of the Interior

NATIONAL PARK SERVICE

Your valued gift

of

A pair of Directoire chairs
for the White House

has been received and is gratefully acknowledged.

To
Mrs. Edythe L. McGinnis *Respectfully yours,*
October 2, 1961.

Conrad L. Wirth
Director, National Park Service

The certificate is similar to those given to all donors. The document labels the chairs as Directoire, a French period immediately preceding Empire, but these are American pieces. Furniture periods overlap, and the labeling of styles are convenient generalizations, rather than scientific descriptions.

Mrs Kennedy beside the Wordsworth Thompson painting of the early Civil War battle of Balls Bluff, Virginia. The painting was acquired by her Committee for Art for the White House.

A discussion with producer, director and commentator. The wire trailing down Mr Collingwood's right leg is a broadcasting antenna. The door leads to the Blue Room.

"Lafayette's March," composed by Miss Caroline Clark for the Boston Independent Cadets. The main theme of the march is a variation on the "Marseillaise." Lafayette's visit to the United States in 1825 was his last. He broke into tears and threw his arms around John Quincy Adams on the eve of his departure. The United States sent him back to France on the warship USS *Brandywine*.

The Blue Room
. . . and the furniture of James Monroe

It had been feared that Mrs Kennedy would be fatigued before the day's work was completed. As the tour went on, she showed increasing enthusiasm and had enough energy for a small dinner party and a view of the recorded tapes. The television crew was far more fatigued than the First Lady.

139

General Badeau.　　General Dent.　　Secretary Fish.　　President Grant.　　Prince Arthur.　　Mr. Thornton.　　Colonel Elphinstone.

The Blue Room in President Grant's time.
　　The room was the traditional setting in which Presidents received the credentials of foreign ambassadors.

140

The Blue Room was used by Grover Cleveland for his marriage to Frances Folsom.
Frances Folsom Cleveland was the youngest woman to serve as First Lady. She
was twenty-two and became one of the most popular women to live in the White
House.

The Blue Room is oval. Because its shape is unusual it has been used for out-of-the-ordinary events. There have been a few attempts in the past to make this room into a comfortable parlor, but they seem not to have succeeded. We are so used to passing our indoor lives within boxes that it is difficult to be at ease in any form that varies from a rectangle. Hoban's oval form would be particularly uncomfortable in a private dwelling, but since the White House needed a room for minor ceremonials, the Blue Room succeeds in announcing them by the curvature of its walls.

The First Floor
As the traditional room for weddings in the White House its first marriage was that of John Adams' niece to his son. Grover Cleveland was the first President to be married in the White House. He wed his ward, Frances Folsom, in the Blue Room.

Again, probably because of the shape of its walls, the Blue Room was the traditional setting in which the President received the credentials of foreign ambassadors. Until 1902 the Blue Room answered the function now served by the Diplomatic Reception Room, one floor below—it was the main south entrance to the building.

Many First Ladies used the room for their receptions. Julia Tyler, Julia Grant, and Lucy Hayes received their guests and answered the duties of protocol in the Blue Room. Mrs Grant, who enjoyed life in the White House to a degree not shared by other *alumnae*, held her weekly receptions from 3 to 5 P.M. "with daylight excluded and soft rays falling from the chandelier above."

Mrs Kennedy's first remark is "under President Monroe, it used to be red. . . ." The tracing of the colors in the Blue Room has been an exercise in scholarship. The room was crimson and gold (the traditional colors of European throne rooms) until Martin Van Buren painted it blue and called it the Elliptical Blue Salon. Various shades of blue are reported: under Grant the room was described as violet-blue; Chester Arthur changed it to robin's egg blue; Mrs Harrison used a figured paper of cerulean blue; Theodore Roosevelt used steel blue; Harry Truman used royal blue; which Mrs Kennedy has temporarily retained. Blue is a cool and formal color: it fits the oval walls and the semi-official nature of the room.

It is tempting to compare the White House with the Kremlin. Both the Soviet Union and the United States had the same problem: how to decorate an official house after a revolution. The Soviet Union receives its formal visitors in the Great Hall of St. George and its antechamber. Though most of the signs of the Tsars have been removed, the double eagles of the Romanovs are ineradicable and the Russians have never changed the gold and crimson of royalty. James Monroe decorated his oval room in the same colors but

142

Entering the Blue Room from the Red Room.   143
    The Blue Room is oval shaped and is used for minor ceremonials and receptions.

blue edged into the room and stayed on. The colors of royalty left the White House long after anti-monarchial fevers had subsided.

The only golden furniture in the White House is in the Blue Room. Mrs Kennedy tells part of the story:

(They enter the Blue Room)

MRS KENNEDY

This room is now blue but, do you know, under President Monroe it used to be red?

The most fascinating thing is this pier table and bust. When we first came here and started searching for old things, we found the pier table in the carpenter shop where it was being used as a sawhorse. And we recognized it from old engravings so we took six weeks to restore it and put it back. And then in the men's room downstairs we found that bust of Washington, which is very primitive. Both sides of his face look different. It was done by an early sculptor. But the interesting thing is these two pieces are exactly where Monroe had them in the room, which we also learned from studying old engravings.

MR COLLINGWOOD

What is this room used for, Mrs Kennedy?

MRS KENNEDY

It's the most formal room in the White House. It's really not used for anything except receiving lines, so all it needs is a table and some beautiful chairs, more to look at than to sit in. The interesting thing about the chairs is that when the picture of the pier table came in the paper, Miss Catherine Bohlen of Villanova, Pennsylvania, sent us a chair, because she recognized that it went with it. It's the only one of the originals that Monroe ordered from Bellangé in Paris. So Charles Francis Adams who is

144

a descendant of Adams, the Adams Presidents, and is on my committee had all the others copied. So now this room looks as it did under Monroe.

MR COLLINGWOOD

You have a wonderful big window here at the end.

MRS KENNEDY

Yes, the view from here is so pretty. You can see the Washington Monument. The interesting thing is that this window used to be the door in olden days. All the carriages would halt at the south entrance and people would come up the stairs because Pennsylvania Avenue wasn't paved until the Civil War. This is where they all came in.

MR COLLINGWOOD

And over on the mantel here, Mrs Kennedy, is this a Monroe piece as well?

MRS KENNEDY

Yes, this is the Minerva clock with candelabras which Monroe also brought from Paris for this room. So you see, everything in it really except the mantel, which is 1902, is Monroe.

(*They exit the Blue Room*)

145

Monroe did not want gilded furniture. The pieces he ordered from France were to be finished in varnished mahogany. This was the style James and Eliza Monroe had seen in the Court of the Emperor Napoleon. By the time Monroe became President, Napoleon had been deposed, and Louis XVIII was the ruler of France. The Bourbons returned to power for a few short years, and one aspect of kingly furniture was revived. The nobility had their furniture gilded, both to announce the return of the royal line and to erase the mahogany style of Napoleon. For this reason, the French supplier wrote a monarchial, snippy letter to the President, stating: "Mahogany is not generally admitted in the furniture of a Saloon, even at private gentlemen's houses." They gilded the mahogany and sent it—but they were respectful enough to remove the crown of Louis XVIII and substitute the American eagle.

Monroe's furniture may have been imported from Europe, but there was one piece in the Blue Room which clearly shows that Europe was receiving strong influences from America. On the southwest curve of the room was a small pencil and sepia drawing titled "Apotheosis of Franklin," done by Jean Honoré Fragonard. Franklin had been Minister Plenipotentiary to France in 1776 and was received with great favor by the Court of Versailles. (Mrs Kennedy moved this sketch to the Green Room after the broadcast.)

The bust of Washington is a minor work by an Italian who carved the President as if he were a Caesar: the Roman nose and the curled hair come straight from Italy's past.

Previously, legend credited this head to Monroe who was supposed to have brought it from Washington's home in Mount Vernon. Shortly after Mrs Kennedy moved into the White House, a search was made of government archives and a receipt was found dating November 11, 1817. The document shows that Benjamin Lear, a Washington dealer, paid $300 for busts of Washington, Columbus, and Amerigo Vespucci. Thus, the exact date and manner in which the artifacts appeared in the White House is established.

The pier table is related to a basic document used for the over-all plan for the Blue Room. When Mrs Kennedy began compiling reference notes on the history of the Executive Mansion she discovered in the January 1946 issue of the *Gazette des Beaux Arts* a reference and a picture of the Monroe pier table. When her search discovered the battered object, she was able to restore the table to its original state. Incidentally, "pier" is the architectural term for the space between two floor-length windows. Pier tables are usually equipped with mirrors along the base for ladies to check their skirts, or to reflect an elaborate carpet.

The original Monroe chair which has been placed beside the pier table is not the only one in existence. Some six others are known, of which two have recently been given to the White House.

This chair dates 1817 and was ordered for the Blue Room by President Monroe. It was given to the White House when the donor recognized that its design matched the pier table to the right. (The chair leg and the table leg are exactly the same design.)

The Minerva clock is another in the collection of Monroe bronzes. The silk damask was placed on the walls in 1952 and will eventually be replaced by Mrs Kennedy.

148

A pencil and sepia drawing "Apotheosis of Franklin" was done by Jean Honoré Fragonard on the occasion of Benjamin Franklin's visit to the Louvre in 1776.

The bust of Washington as a Caesar.

A search of government archives turned up this receipt, showing that the Washington bust was one of three sold for $100 each by Benjamin Lear, a Washington dealer. This receipt disproves the story that Monroe brought the bust from Washington's home in Mount Vernon.

The Green Room
. . . and Federal furniture

Entering the Green Room.

The table in the right background gives the key to the room. It is an original Federal piece dating 1800, and was one of the two antiques in the room. Previously the room had been furnished with copies or imitations of late eighteenth-century furniture.

Mrs Kennedy's innovations can be seen on the table: the ash tray and flowers. She has said that she wanted to give the White House a "lived-in look." When she was a child she visited the building and was taken aback by its "museum-like feeling."

151

(They enter the Green Room)

The First Floor

MRS KENNEDY

This is what an American parlor would have looked like at the time of Adams and Jefferson—a room dating 1800. When we came these were the only two antique pieces of furniture in the room; this pair of card tables. As we hate to change we decided that we would let them dictate the style of the room. But the funny thing about them is—you know Henry Du Pont who is chairman of my committee and established Winterthur, he noticed them right away and said, "These are the only good things in the room, I wonder who gave them?" It turned out it was his sister, Mrs Crowninshield.

MR COLLINGWOOD

What other objects of special interest are there in the room now?

MRS KENNEDY

Well, there's this sofa which belonged to Daniel Webster and is really one of the finest pieces in this room. And then there's this mirror. It was George Washington's and he had it in the Executive Mansion in Philadelphia, then he gave it to a friend and it was there until Mount Vernon lent it to us this fall. And I must say I appreciate that more than I can say, because when Mount Vernon, which is probably the most revered house in this country, lends something to the White House, you know they have confidence that it will be taken care of.

MR COLLINGWOOD

And that's a magnificent desk under it.

152

The south side of the Green Room on the day of broadcast.

On the following page the reader will find Mrs Kennedy's description of the desk. Since she made her remarks the piece has been taken apart and discovered to be a reproduction—not an antique.

153

At the time this photograph was taken everyone thought the desk to be genuine. The donor, the recipient, and most of the experts dated the desk as authentic Federal—about 1800. Subsequent research established that the piece had been manufactured at least eighty years later.

As most antique collectors know, the dating of old pieces is still an art, and not yet a science!

MRS KENNEDY

Yes, that has a fascinating story too. That was our first piece of unsolicited fine furniture. One day Mrs Maurice Noun from Des Moines, Iowa, came into the Curator's Office and asked us if we would like to have it. It turns out there are only four like it in existence: in the Metropolitan, in Winterthur, and in the Maryland Historical Society. It's a Baltimore lady's desk made only in Baltimore—classical with sandalwood inlay, and eglomise panels, which is gold painting on glass. It's really a treasure and I wish there were more people like Mrs Noun because it is hard to get people to part with fine furniture.

MR COLLINGWOOD

One of the nicest things in this room to my untutored eye is that portrait of a beautiful young lady over the fireplace.

MRS KENNEDY

You're right. It's one of the best pictures in the White House. It's Angelica Van Buren who was a Southern girl, Van Buren's daughter-in-law. She was his hostess. It's by Henry Inman. It really is terribly good.

MR COLLINGWOOD

Is that Van Buren himself in the picture—the bust?

MRS KENNEDY

That's a bust of him, yes, which is another one we found. And on the mantel is the Monroe Hannibal clock and two Monroe vases.

154   (*They exit the Green Room*)

The east side of the Green Room.

The mantelpiece has a twin in the Red Room. Both were ordered in 1817 by James Hoban. Above the fireplace is the portrait of Angelica Van Buren. Since the broadcast this painting has been replaced by one of Benjamin Franklin.

The pair of settees flanking the fireplace are Federal and have been covered with a fabric copying an early nineteenth-century design. The thinness and delicacy of the woodworking is a sign of the excellent craftsmanship of the Federal cabinet-makers.

155

Since Mrs Kennedy made the remarks quoted above, the portrait of Angelica Van Buren has been replaced by a portrait of Benjamin Franklin. The George Washington mirror has also been moved. Other changes are contemplated. It all recalls the axiom that the White House is a home; like other American houses its changes are continual.

Thomas Jefferson used this room as a dining room. To avoid the question of who sat at the head of the table when the President was present, Mr Jefferson used a round table. He also installed revolving trays in the wall so that the servants could remain in the pantry and thus not hear what was being discussed. President Jefferson's inventiveness was also culinary: he imported recipes for waffles and macaroni, and introduced ice cream made according to a notation which he had brought from France.

When Monroe refurnished the White House he covered the chairs in green silk and hung green draperies over white dimity. From then on tradition kept the color in the room, although ladies in Jackson's time are reported to have thought the color odious because it made their complexions seem sallow. President Monroe called the room "The Card Room"; he and his friends used it after dinner for card games.

In later administrations there were attempts to make the Green Room cozy and homelike. It became a place for small social meetings and family gatherings. The furniture flowed in and out: Mary Lincoln used rosewood and ebony furniture covered with green and gold brocatelle. Chester Arthur hung new green silk curtains over white fringed muslin. The walls were covered with paper—in Victorian times the paper was heavily patterned, but Mrs Harrison began a new trend, using a plain pale green. The 1902 restoration revived the French influence of placing fabric on the walls. A green Genoese velvet covered the walls. Mrs Coolidge used a soft green damask; the Trumans replaced the damask with green silk brocade which still remains.

When President Truman restored the White House he found the original Hoban cornices which had been buried under the elaborate plaster work of later administrations. The Hoban cornices were copied for the present room, but the ceiling was lowered to make room for air conditioning ducts.

Mrs Kennedy has chosen 1800 as the date for the room. She has placed Federal furniture throughout—but it is obvious that the Green Room is not to be a museum. The Federal pieces are to be a base against which many decorative ideas can be worked. It must be remembered that none of the pieces in the room were in the White House in 1800, thus she has the opportunity to select the best antiques of the period for the décor. The sofa which belonged to Daniel Webster is an American adaptation of a Sheraton style. It is a perfect example of the kinds of pieces which Mrs Kennedy is seeking: its lines fit the Green Room, and it has historical value because Daniel Webster was a constant White House visitor for some forty years.

The Federal period of American furniture has always attracted a great deal of interest. It is the earliest design which would fit the White House. There are American designs which precede the Federal period, but either they are so close to English pieces as to be unsuitable, or as in the case of colonial inventions, they are too crude for a public room. Most experts take the American Revolution as a convenient starting date for Federal lines. Additionally, a single cabinetmaker had a great influence on furniture: Duncan Phyfe reached his greatest period in the early 1800s.

Like everything else in the Revolutionary era, Federal finds its roots in Europe. It is a mixture of Louis XVI, Directoire, Sheraton, and local American influences. Mrs Kennedy's Green Room is in the early period of Federal when English styles were still admissible. Later, as anti-British sentiment swept the country, there was a deliberate attempt to eliminate British lines from the furniture. Most experts classify Federal furniture as the best design in our history.

There are many reasons why Federal furniture was popular in post-Revolutionary America and why it was a favorite design of George Washington, Thomas Jefferson, and John Adams. President Adams left an inventory of his White House furnishings in 1801. His inventory shows no furnishings of the Chippendale period or earlier, nor satinwood furniture nor French marquetry pieces. None of these styles are included in the Federal. They are elaborations foreign to the spirit of the American Revolution. Marquetry was a sign of royalty, and therefore unsuitable to the White House or the spirit of the times.

Of course no one sat down and wrote a list of unacceptable decorations for the White House. Questions of taste cannot be examined too closely. But the questions of taste in Revolutionary times have their parallels today. Without detailing the reasons, it would seem sacrilegious to decorate the Green Room in foam, formica, and fluorescent. In a parallel mood the early Revolutionaries discarded the obvious signs of monarchy.

This only explains what is not in the Green Room, and not in the Federal period. It is tempting to look at the pieces which Mrs Kennedy has gathered and find in them the social causes of the American Revolution. Analysis can be made, but the relationship between philosophy and furniture cannot be expressed in more than general opinions.

The furniture is simple in design, rational in proportion, and without ostentation. It is not difficult to equate these virtues with the American Revolution. The thinness of the legs and the careful cabinetwork of every piece in the room could only be evolved in small workshops set up for patient

157

hand carving: again, this announces a social system after the ornateness of royalty and before the machine age.

In the Green Room richness comes out of simplicity: the tenet is Jeffersonian, and the room is in the style of Thomas Jefferson's personal furniture. Those who see a chair solely as something to sit on may become impatient with such analysis. It must be frankly admitted that these parallels seem more apparent in hindsight. But the similarities have occurred to more than a few people who have seen the Green Room. The whole argument underlies the sciences that study the past. Archeologists and anthropologists construct the pattern of whole civilizations from artifacts.

Of all the rooms of the White House, today's Green Room matches best the mood of the architect, James Hoban. The tourist who looks into it sees the Green Room as more cool than dramatic, more rational than sensual. The Green Room is Federal America.

The First Floor

(*They enter the Main Corridor from Green Room*)

MR COLLINGWOOD

Mrs Kennedy, we've now seen the State Rooms of the White House. But the Lincoln Room is upstairs. Could we see that?

MRS KENNEDY

Yes, that's a very special room, you should see that.

MR COLLINGWOOD

This staircase goes up to the second floor which is reserved for the private living of the President and his family. I don't think any television or motion picture cameras have ever gone up there, because that's where you live. But in President Lincoln's day the offices were there.

MRS KENNEDY

That's right. I'm glad they're not now.

158   (*They start upstairs to second floor*)

Until 1902 the public had access to the second floor by means of this staircase. A visitor once wrote: "The atmosphere is close and heavy on this staircase. . . . Perhaps the sighs of the disappointed office seekers who for more than half a century have descended the steps give to the air a quality that defies ventilation. All these people are eager-eyed, restless and nervous. They want something which the great man . . . can give if he chooses, but which they fear they will not get."

159

"In Lincoln's time the stairway to his office was always crowded with friends, job seekers, and cronies. They climbed the stairs and came down the stairs, having had their moment with the President.

"Here is what the White House did to President Lincoln. Here is how he changed. 1861. The strong man with the arched eyebrow. 1865. One week before his assassination."

FIRST LADIES

Martha Washington

Abigail Adams

Louisa Adams

Martha Dandridge Custis Washington who never lived in the White House, but who established its early protocol.

Abigail Quincy Smith Adams, the only woman whose husband and son were Presidents of the United States.

Louisa Catherine Johnson Adams had definite opinions about "popular governments."

Gold and blue are the sole colors of the Blue Room.

THE second floor of the White House is reserved for the private use of the President and his family. Guarded day and night by Secret Service personnel, it is a refuge which every incoming President tries to keep for himself. Here public life becomes private, and for a few hours each day the President can withdraw from his official duties. In the White House, the second floor is home. The lines of tourists do not pass through the family quarters, and the official life of the President enters the second floor only as he desires. Tradition has made this floor the domain of the President's wife.

History marches officially through the State Rooms downstairs. One floor below are the Public rooms and public pronouncements. But the second floor is private, and the First Lady is a private citizen who has not been elected to her office. It is a place of confidences; thus, the story of the women who have occupied the apartments on this floor is difficult to piece together.

There are no rules, only patterns. Including Mrs Kennedy, some forty women since Abigail Adams have had influence over the ways of the White House. They made do, or they made over. They participated, or they withdrew. None was raised to be the wife of the President. Young, old; timid, sharp; beautiful, ugly; daughters, mothers, grandmothers; fashionable, ordinary—all the stages of women passed through the White House. Their progression does not follow the political history of the United States. The great themes of the development of a continent have little to do with the selection of a First Lady. Nor do the women of the White House follow the succession of styles, as do the furnishings.

Yet there are patterns. The most general is predictable: on the second floor of the White House most wives have tried to live a normal family life. Before all, they were mothers and wives. Only if it were necessary to participate in White House affairs would they do so. From Elizabeth Monroe to Mamie Eisenhower, runs a sporadic pattern of women who attended only the most necessary ceremonials. Arriving late, they said little, and departed early. They frustrated the official reporters, refused to leave anecdotes, and completely detached themselves from their husband's public life. They exercised their privilege of privacy—and America respected them for it.

This major theme of concern for husband and family was best expressed (as might be expected) through a quotation by a second person. President

163

Taylor said his wife "made a nightly prayer that Henry Clay might be elected in my place." At least one wife has regarded the whole business as a prison sentence, and, like a convict, kept her eye on the next Inauguration Day. Most women have worried about their husband's health. The rate of mortality is high, and the rapid aging of Presidents is a matter of photographic record.

Nevertheless, the President is somewhat prepared for the White House. No man has ever been elected who didn't want the job. A presidential campaign has never been won without a struggle, and politics is a teacher. There is no school for wives: the President's wife is without title. The press has given her the unofficial title of "The First Lady" or "The Official Hostess." Whether from the backwoods or Back Bay, the wives are expected to run the White House with elegance, taste, and tact. The requirement has frightened at least a half-dozen wives into real or imaginary illnesses. This pattern of an ill wife was a strong tradition in the middle of the nineteenth century.

First Ladies

A third pattern is that of queenliness. It has been out of vogue during this century, but could reappear. Another is that of a wife strongly involved in politics. Finally (as a subdivision of the pattern of domesticity), there is a repeated theme of the wife who knows nothing of politics. (Some wives did not know the names of the members of their husbands' Cabinet.)

One further observation: the reporting of the President's wife has itself developed a tradition. At the beginning of any administration every First Lady is automatically "gracious and modest." The male reader wandering through the pages of early reporting is well advised to learn the art of reading the unwritten—like studying the pronouncements of the Kremlin. The best way is to wait for the next administration to take over, and then note the remarks entitled "Changes in the White House."

As an example, the contemporary reporting of the first two Presidents' wives flowered with descriptions of "sensitive ladies"—"proud of their husbands" who made his surroundings "dignified, rational but republican." It is only when Dolley Madison enters the White House that we learn from the same reporter that "the forms and ceremonials which had rendered the drawing rooms of Mrs Washington and Mrs Adams dull and tedious were laid aside."

Martha Washington never lived in the White House; nevertheless, the first First Lady left a sentence which all who followed her would recognize: "Indeed I think I am more like a State prisoner than anything else." She called the "Father of Our Country" her "old man," but she was exercising aristocratic privilege rather than speaking colloquially. A rich widow, she married George Washington in 1759. As an elderly lady she had a fine sense of ceremony.

164

Mrs Washington had to lay down the first rules of protocol—another theme

Dolley Payne Todd Madison, the first exception to all the rules.   165

that runs through the history of First Ladies. She and her husband set some simple rules. The President had it be known:

"He would receive anyone who had any formal business with the President of the United States every other Tuesday between three and four. The only provision was that the visitor be known to his Secretary or some gentleman whom the President knew.

"The President received formal visitors in front of the fireplace with his face towards the door. His hair was in full dress; he held a cocked hat; he wore knee and shoe buckles and a long sword. The visitor was conducted to him and he required to have the name so distinctly pronounced that he could hear it. He bowed and would not shake hands, even with his closest friends, that no distinction might be made. Mrs Washington received her visitors in two formal rooms. On the evenings when Mrs Washington received visitors, he did not consider himself as visited. He was then a private gentleman, with neither hat nor sword.

"He had once a fortnight an official dinner. He sat at the side in a central position, Mrs Washington opposite."

Martha Washington's successor was a close friend, Abigail Adams, who lived in the White House for only a short period. Several themes started with her. She had spent a good deal of time in Europe at the Court of St. James's, and much admired protocol as a means of protection and privacy. Additionally, she had a good grasp of politics. It is reported that "John always discussed affairs of state with her. Often, listening to her opinions and forthright ideas, he saw conditions more clearly and was influenced by her sound judgment." As the reader will see, this pattern of wifely helpfulness with affairs of state will be repeated—with some unexpected consequences—over the next century and a half.

Mrs Adams was the only woman whose son and husband were both Presidents of the United States. She worked hard to set the social tone of the presidency. It is ironic that in legend Abigail Adams is known as the woman who had her laundry dried in the East Room—in fact, she was an intellectual and a social leader of great skill who made certain that the rules of protocol were obeyed. As early as 1790, when her husband was George Washington's Secretary of State, Mrs Adams wrote:

"My station is always at the right hand of Mrs Washington. I find it sometimes occupied, but on such occasions the President never fails to see that it is relinquished for me. Having removed ladies several times, they have now learned to rise up and give it to me."

The same sense of the propriety of ceremony was brought into the White House and remained there until John Adams left the building.

Thomas Jefferson couldn't have cared less. A widower, and a ferocious disbeliever in rank, he prohibited "gentlemen offering their arms to ladies and going into dinner in any order or rank or honor." His two daughters were raising families in Virginia, and the role of First Lady was not as important to President Jefferson as it had been to Mrs Adams. When he needed a hostess at the White House, he sent a messenger to the wife of his Secretary of State, James Madison: "Thomas Jefferson begs Mrs Madison to take care of female friends expected—"

So enters Dolley Madison, the first exception to all the rules. She was an influence in the White House longer than any other woman. She answered Thomas Jefferson's note in 1801. She was the official hostess during the eight years Jefferson was President, and the eight years her husband served. She was a force in the White House until her death in 1849.

Dolley's first husband was a Philadelphia lawyer who died of smallpox. Her next marriage—to James Madison—seems to have been arranged by Martha Washington, although there is a story that she preferred Aaron Burr. She had a personality which hardly suited the earnestness of the times. It is better described by anecdote than analysis.

The British papers called her "The American Queen." Dolley wore fashionable gowns, turbans—and took snuff. She once offered Henry Clay a pinch from an ornate box and took some herself. She then pulled a bandanna from her pocket and said, "Mr Clay, this is for rough work and this"—drawing a fine lace handkerchief from another pocket—"is my polisher."

Probably no other woman presided with the same flair and brilliance. Her wit and manners attracted men, but she was not so beautiful as to evoke jealousy. Her dresses were elegant, but had been made in the world of the possible. The ladies rallied around her. Everyone writes about her zest and innocence. Innocent or not, she knew how to win feuds and influence people. So long as a woman touches politics, she might as well succeed at both. Her finest hour was at the expense of British Minister Anthony Merry and his wife. Mr Merry (who sounds like the kind of diplomat Britain no longer exports) found America "a thousand times worse than the worst parts of Spain" and after dining at the Madison home called the meal "more like a harvest home supper than the entertainment of a Secretary of State." Dolley's answer recalls Jane Austen: she thought "abundance was preferable to elegance; that circumstances formed customs and customs formed taste. The profusion arose from the happy circumstance of the prosperity of our country. I did not hesitate to sacrifice the delicacy of European taste for the less elegant but more liberal fashions of Virginia."

In the days when twisting the Lion's tail was a national sport, Dolley had scored well.

Dolley began the tradition of egg rolling on the Monday after Easter. The children of Washington used the Capitol lawn for this ancient Egyptian game. Later, the tradition would be moved to the White House lawn.

After Dolley, there was less fun in the White House. Elizabeth Monroe was a serene aristocrat who delegated most of her duties to her daughter. (Later wives would use Mrs Monroe's example as a happy precedent.) Both Mrs Monroe and her daughter, Eliza Hay, showed slight symptoms of Queen fever. There was much to do about who called on whom, and who walked into a room before somebody else. These two ladies and their successor, Louisa Catherine Adams, thought a good deal of form and very little of substance. Mrs Hay boycotted the whole Diplomatic Corps. Monroe's Cabinet, with the exception of the Secretary of State, boycotted his drawing rooms. One poor relative was turned away from the White House because he came to dinner in trousers instead of knee breeches and silk stockings.

It all fit the temper of the times; there was a political and cultural lag between Washington and the rest of the country which would end only when Andrew Jackson came to power.

But the subject is Queen fever. Both Monroe and Adams served as Secretaries of State, and as Ministers to the Court of St. James's and the Court of France. Mrs Adams had observed the Russian Court at St. Petersburg, which was more French and ceremonial than the Court of Louis XVI had ever been. The ladies probably thought they were acting with republican simplicity. In all honesty, it must be said that about this time the European Ambassadors to Washington still treated the United States as an afterthought of European civilization. Nevertheless, Mrs Hay sent an announcement to the French Ambassador which is hardly equivalent to Dolley Madison's retort to Ambassador Merry. Mrs Hay wrote in the third person singular:

"Against her will she would go to the ball next Monday, but it was upon conditions: first, that it should leave her position with the ladies of the foreign Ministers precisely where it was; that she would afterwards neither visit them, nor receive visits from them. At supper she would find her place somewhere, but must have no particular distinction shown her. If an account of the ball was to be published in the newspapers here, her name should not be mentioned as having been present."

Aside from violating the First Amendment, the statement has an imperiousness which would not be matched until Louisa Adams attacked the opposition

Letitia Tyler

Julia Tyler

Sarah Polk

Letitia Christian Tyler was an invalid and died during her husband's term of office.
Julia Gardiner Tyler was young, extravagant and had a bad case of queen fever.
Sarah Childress Polk was her husband's private secretary.

169

Angelica Singleton Van Buren served as official hostess for her father-in-law, Martin Van Buren.

to her husband. The following quotation needs decoding: "Popular governments" means the movement toward political equality for those free people who did not own property; "demagogue" is Andrew Jackson, and "old and faithful servant" is of course her husband. But the statement has faint praise for the democratic process:

"Popular governments are peculiarly liable to factions, to cabals, to intrigue. The people may often be deceived for a time by some fair-speaking demagogue, but they will never be deceived long. Though they may, in a moment of excitement, sanction an injustice toward an old and faithful servant, they appreciate his worth."

The last Tsarina wrote in a similar style when she discussed Nicholas II and the peasants of Russia.

John Quincy Adams left the White House. Andrew Jackson who followed him was a widower who did not attach much importance to the role of First Lady. A number of his female relatives served as official hostesses, and Queenliness departed from the social scene for eight years.

It returned during Martin Van Buren's administration. Van Buren was a dapper, fussy widower with four sons, and in 1837 Dolley Madison was still a force in Washington. Among her other accomplishments was matchmaking. She paired off Abraham Van Buren, the President's son, with Angelica Singleton, one of Dolley's relatives. Angelica and husband were sent off on the Grand Tour, with special emphasis on London where they saw Queen Victoria crowned. Angelica came back to reign as the President's official hostess.

Queen fever has two outward symptoms. The first is to sit down while receiving guests, which Angelica did not quite dare do. The second is to wear a crown, and Angelica did it, but in code. She put three feathers in a jeweled headdress, and although other ladies of the time copied the fashion, all saw to it that their plumes were slightly shorter.

President William Henry Harrison's wife never got into the White House (he died before she could get there), and John Tyler's first wife was an invalid who died after he took office.

Between the death of his first wife and the marriage to his second, President Tyler appointed the task of hostess to his daughter-in-law, Priscilla. She had played bit parts (her father was a famous tragedian) and on arrival she saw the White House as a marvelous setting. A letter to her sister echoes every young actress who has found a good role:

171

"Here am I . . . actually living in, or, what is more, presiding at the White House! . . .

"I really do possess a degree of modest assurance that surprises me more than it does any one else. I am complimented on every side; my hidden virtues are coming out. I am considered 'charmante' by the Frenchmen, 'lovely' by the Americans, and 'really quite nice, you know,' by the English. . . . I have had some lovely dresses made which fit me to perfection—one a pearl-colored silk that will set you crazy."

Later, the actress gives way to the mother.

"My first state dinner is over; oh! such a long one. I was the only lady at the table. I tried to be as cheerful as possible, though I felt miserable all the time, as my baby was crying and I received message after message to come to the nursery."

John Tyler's second wife was one of the most beautiful women to reign in the White House. "Reign" is the proper verb for her ambitions. Julia Tyler was young, extravagant, and had Queen fever to a degree never repeated again. A contemporary account recalls: "Her serene loveliness receives upon a raised platform wearing a headdress resembling a crown. She received seated on a slightly raised platform." Julia Tyler went even further. She appointed twelve ladies in waiting who stood around the dais, while the wife of the President conducted her audience in a purple dress.

For the next twelve years, the White House went into a slow decline. Mrs Polk received seated, wearing heavy velvet dresses, but she did not have her mind on social behavior. She was her husband's private secretary and exerted a strong political influence on the President. Extremely religious and a good business woman, she had little gaiety in her personality. The only flurries in the White House were caused by the appearance of the venerable Dolley Madison, who visited the President's house often. Although she was eighty-two years old, at the time of her last visit she wore a décolleté gown to show that her arms and shoulders were still beautiful.

Zachary Taylor's wife was an invalid who delegated her authority to her young daughter. Mrs Taylor's premonition of her husband's death in the White House was correct. She left the White House and never spoke of it again, except as connected with the death of her husband.

Mrs Fillmore was a former school teacher who had tutored her husband. She was older than the President, with strong intellectual and religious leanings. Abigail Fillmore disliked the social duties expected of a President's wife, and delegated as much authority as possible to her daughter. She received Washington Irving and William Thackeray, put a library in the White House, and avoided public appearances.

Abigail Fillmore was succeeded by Jane Pierce. Her view of the White House was expressed the first moment she heard that she might become its mistress. She and her husband were returning from a visit to a Massachusetts cemetery when a messenger told them that the deadlocked Democratic convention had selected Franklin Pierce. Mrs Pierce fainted.

She was tubercular; her husband was a reformed alcoholic. She hated Washington so much that she could not bear to appear as official hostess until twenty-two months after her husband was inaugurated. Her surrogate was Mrs Abby Kent Means, a friend and distant relative. Pious, retiring, painfully shy, Mrs Pierce left the White House so ill that she had to be carried.

For twelve years the White House had been gray. Three successive wives had been ill, and the center of the social world had shifted from the Executive Mansion. When James Buchanan entered the building he was a bachelor who appointed his ward, Harriet Lane, as his official hostess.

Buchanan was a weak and vacillating President. But Harriet Lane was a beautiful, imperious girl of twenty-four who meant to revive the White House. She had Queen fever, and her uncle obviously enjoyed the brilliant festivities she instituted. Jefferson Davis summed it up neatly some years later, writing in a prison cell:

"The White House under the administration of Buchanan approached more nearly to my idea of a Republican court than the President's house has ever done before."

Harriet Lane did the grandest tour possible. She was a favorite of Queen Victoria, and when her uncle and Tennyson received degrees at Oxford "her appearance was greeted with loud cheers by the students and murmurs of admiration." At the White House she received seated (but without a dais), she wore a headdress, she introduced Victoria's dress to society, and the President's house became a hotel for visiting royalty. The Prince of Wales stopped overnight (but Buchanan, who would not permit dancing in the Executive Mansion, sent him off to waltz at the British Ministry). The first Japanese diplomatic staff and the Prince de Joinville, son of Louis Philippe of France, were honored guests. Harriet Lane was exquisite, acted with political sagacity in aiding her uncle, and had perfect taste for her time.

From Monroe through Buchanan, the "let's-play-Queen" school of White House hostesses echoed the aristocratic South and the courts of Europe.

Abigail Fillmore

Martha Patterson

Abigail Powers Fillmore had strong intellectual leanings.

Martha Johnson Patterson, Andrew Johnson's daughter and hostess, who wrote: "I trust that too much will not be expected from us."

Harriet Lane was President Buchanan's niece and hostess. She revived the White House after twelve years of elderly or invalid First Ladies.

Their pretentions constituted no internal threat to the security of the United States, and no social threat to reigning European monarchs. In the minute mutation of American life that regarded itself as High Society, there was always the sentiment that while the American Revolution was proper, it was crude. Cutting off from the British was one thing; cutting off from a Crown was another. Alas, we did, and forevermore there was no Central Social Authority. Ambitious daughters might marry European titles, but like some European wines, they lost authority in travel. This mild social disease, whose primary symptom is centralized correctness, still survives in disguised forms like Debutantism.

First Ladies

Ordinary Americans didn't know who Harriet Lane or Julia Tyler were imitating. They knew something simpler and more important: they have always recognized that the First Lady was the President's choice, not theirs.

The great exception was Mary Todd Lincoln.

Excluding a social snip here and a column there, the women of the White House have been criticized only mildly while they are in residence, and suffer only by comparison once they have become *alumnae*. But the viciousness of the attack against Mary Lincoln began before she reached the White House, continued unabated during her stay, and pursued her to her death.

Her very appearance alienated the Court Reporters. Harriet Lane moved, almost by reflex, through the best tradition of English, French, and Virginia fashion. Mary Lincoln was from provincial Midwest society. A product of a border state, she was attacked for her relatives who were fighting with the Confederacy. She lost a son to typhoid in the White House; yet her mourning was too intense for everyone. The grief for the death of her favorite son was itself a device by which she could be attacked. "Mrs Lincoln had the privilege of seeing her son die, instead of having to send him out to be shot on a battlefield."

Above all, she was extravagant. She spent a fortune she did not have on her clothes. Her mourning dress was itself a good example. "I want the *very finest* and blackest and lightest long crepe veil. Please get the finest that can be obtained. I want a very, very fine black crepe veil, round corners and folds around . . ."

Before Lincoln's re-election she said: "I have contracted large debts of which he knows nothing." (The debt was about $27,000.) "Mr Lincoln has but little idea of the expense of a woman's wardrobe. He is happy in the belief that the few hundred dollars I obtain from him supply all my wants. If he knew his wife was involved to the extent she is, the knowledge would

176

drive him mad. If he is re-elected, I can keep him in ignorance of my affairs, but if he is defeated, then the bills will be sent in and he will know all."

The papers lashed at her.

"At the White House, a lonely man, bearing the Nation's fate upon his shoulders, lived and toiled and suffered alone. His wife during all the summer was at the hotels of fashionable watering places.

"Every railroad train that entered the city bore fresh troops to the Nation's rescue and fresh mourners seeking the dead. Through it all, Mrs. Lincoln 'shopped.'"

She never had enough money for herself, but she never stopped shopping. She spent $2000 for her second inaugural gown. After Lincoln's death, to raise funds for her supposed indebtedness, she had a sale in New York of some eighteen dresses and other items. A bolt of fine lace for $4000, a shawl at $2000 but nothing was sold. Her closest confidante was her dressmaker, Elizabeth Keckley, who had been a slave and from whom Mrs Lincoln would order twelve dresses at a time. Mrs Keckley's ghostwritten book told all.

Mary Todd Lincoln was not only extravagant for herself; she overspent on redecorating the White House while the country was at war. She was afraid her husband would be angry and she asked that the bills be kept from him. She urged that the President be told it was "common to overrun appropriations."

But Major French, the Commissioner of Public Buildings, told Lincoln, who was furious. "It can never have my approval. I'll pay it out of my own pocket first. It would stink in the nostrils of the American people to have it said the President of the United States approved a bill overrunning an appropriation for flub-dubs for this damned old house, when the soldiers cannot have blankets." Major French's journal tells this story.

Everybody wrote a book—except Mary Lincoln.

She was not only extravagant; she expected others to pay her way. "The Republican politicians must pay my debts. Hundreds of them are getting immensely rich off the patronage of my husband, and it is but fair they should help me out of my embarrassment."

It has all been documented.

It went on, even after she left the White House. She claimed that she was destitute and needed a pension. By 1868 Lincoln's estate had increased to $110,000 of which her portion was a third. Some $10,000 had been given to her by public subscription. Congress first gave her $22,000 as a year's presidential salary. Later—after some debate—she was voted an annual

177

Mary Todd Lincoln.

pension of $5000. In 1875 she was found to be carrying $57,000 in securities in her pocket. It was then she was declared insane.

Until her death, she claimed she had no money, and the country had been ungrateful.

The worst charge was put directly:

"The match was an unfortunate one. It united two people of widely divergent taste and characteristics."

There are fashions in the reporting of history, and for a hundred years it has been fashionable to write of this woman in hushed, shocked tones. But political analysis, modern psychiatry, and poetic insight have today started a slow swing to sympathy for Mary Todd Lincoln. She was undeniably a little mad, but today the logic of madness is better understood.

In her lifetime she looked for help; she consulted mediums. Yet how great a bridge was this from her husband? He reports that one night he threw himself on a couch and saw himself in a mirror:

"I saw myself reflected. But my face, I noticed, had two separate and distinct images. The tip of the nose of one being about three inches from the tip of the other. I noticed that one of the faces was a little paler, say five shades, than the other. I got up and went off.

"Now and again the thing would come up and give me a little pang, as though something uncomfortable had happened.

"I never succeeded in bringing the ghost back after that.

"My wife was worried about it. She thought it was a sign that I was to be elected to a second term of office. The paleness of one of the faces was an omen that I should not see life through the second term."

Whatever their private world, they lived in it together.

As for the public world, so filled with her extravagances, it turns out that there is an excuse here and there. Her private bills were, in all fairness, her private matter. The charge that she overspent on White House furnishings, yields before documentation. She was only given $20,000. Their predecessor, Buchanan, spent $25,000 on furniture. Directly after the Lincolns, Johnson would spend $30,000 on the building, and Ulysses S. Grant would spend $250,000.

Later the charge became that Mrs Lincoln had carted away furniture from the White House and sold it. With the growth of the Lincoln legend, this story has been seized upon by any number of dealers in Americana. The numbers and sizes of the boxes supposedly sent from the White House have grown through the years. The facts seem to be that Mrs Lincoln was as compulsive about saving as she was about spending. Mrs Keckley reports that aside from trunks, Mrs Lincoln left with some fifty or sixty boxes of personal objects and private gifts sent to the White House. Mary Lincoln later gave a detailed list of the contents of the boxes, pointing out that she had given some items to charity fairs in Chicago. The only piece of public furniture she took was a small dressing stand, and for that she had the permission of the Commissioner of Public Buildings. The present archivist of the Lincoln Museum, Stanley McClure, has a record of every auction held by White House occupants. There is no evidence of Mrs Lincoln removing any of the furniture.

What lay behind the attacks? Politics for one excuse.

Lincoln had been elected because of a split in the Democratic party. To preserve the unity of the Republican party he offered high Cabinet positions to four of his rivals: Seward, Secretary of State; Chase, Secretary of the Treasury; Bates, Attorney General; Cameron, Secretary of War, later replaced by Stanton. Chase and Stanton were after the 1864 nomination. As a wartime President and leader of the party, Lincoln could only be attacked on the flanks. Chase, whose campaign was to be the most intense, concentrated on a radical Abolition position to come around the left flank, and sent his daughter Kate, a brilliant, beautiful woman, around the right. She set up a deliberate social rivalry which did not end when Lincoln appointed her father to the Supreme Court. Kate Chase had gone so far as to hold her own court in the Blue Room while the President's wife was receiving in the East Room. Chase's encircling movement failed, but Mrs Lincoln was a casualty.

The scandals of profiteering in the Civil War have been fully documented. Speculation, shoddy matériel of war, and no substantial limitation of profits led to overnight fortunes.

All wars have inequality of sacrifice. To those who stayed home, prospered and propagandized, what better way to exorcize guilt than to attack a mad, headstrong, and extravagant woman?

She was vulnerable for many reasons. Her physical appearance was against her. Lincoln was tall, lean, gaunt, threadbare. The President's wife stood beside him; chubby, in high color, and dressed in the protection she so obviously needed; his simplicity made her furbelows the more rococo. The North needed his saintliness, but saints ought not be married. The White House was the set, Lincoln was the hero, and in dramatic terms, the greater his trials, the higher and more purging his tragedy. America needed a villainess, and Mary Lincoln was fully costumed. She served her country, but the need she served was dark.

After Mary Lincoln, domesticity returned to the White House. The attention of the country no longer centered on the wife of the President. Andrew Johnson faced a political story which did not touch his infirm wife or his acting hostess, Martha Patterson. Perhaps Mrs Patterson had Mrs Lincoln on her mind when she wrote:

"We are plain people from the mountains of Tennessee called here for a short time. I trust that too much will not be expected from us."

President Johnson's wife appeared only once in public. At a reception for her grandchildren she remained seated and said: "My dears, I am an invalid." Her daughter repaired the White House, but the Executive Mansion was no longer the center of Washington Society.

The crown had fallen to Julia Grant, even before her husband was elected. Unlike many of her predecessors, Mrs Grant was happy in the White House, she wrote:

"My life at the White House was a bright and beautiful dream . . . Life at the White House was a garden spot of orchids. I wish it might have continued forever . . . a feast of cleverness and wit, with men who were the brainiest their states and countries could send, and women unrivalled anywhere for beauty, talent and tact."

Julia Grant had once been attacked by Mary Lincoln, who had said to her sharply: "I suppose you think you'll get to the White House yourself, don't you?" The lady journalists who rose during Abolition times were still attacking Mrs Lincoln. They damned her by praising Julia Grant. One wrote:

"The moral atmosphere of the Presidential Mansion has been a matter of congratulation to the American people. They do not forget that the personal influence of Mrs Grant had much to do with impressing this characteristic of her husband's administration upon the world at large."

The moral atmosphere of the Grant administration was so bad that Henry Adams (a slightly more sensitive reporter) went abroad for a year to take a "moral bath." Julia Grant was oblivious to the scandals. Her afternoon receptions re-established the social dominance of the White House.

When President Grant left the White House, the United States was ready for an administration of reform and self-denial. Lucy Hayes fit her times.

181

Someone got drunk at an early reception for two obscure Russians and until the Hayes administration ended, liquor was forbidden. The criticisms were minor, male, and heartfelt. They called her "Lemonade Lucy." A reporter commented sadly, "Water flows like wine in the White House."

(The Women's Christian Temperance Union stood foursquare behind Mrs Hayes. In appreciation of a dry White House, they gave her a fine sideboard. The sideboard was sold in one of the later auctions of White House furniture. In the administration of Franklin Roosevelt, a congressman reported indignantly that the sideboard was being used in a Washington saloon.)

The virtues of the Midwest and particularly Ohio were now better understood by lady journalists. Austere, dignified, maternal, Lucy Hayes was accepted by Mary Clemmer who had attacked Mary Lincoln.

On Inauguration Day, 1877, Miss Clemmer saw the Midwestern future and set up a defense for Lucy Hayes against the eastern fashion editors.

"I have never seen such a face reign in the White House. I wonder what the world of Vanity Fair will do with it? Will it frizz that hair?—powder that face?—draw those sweet fine lines away with pride?"

Garfield was shot, and Chester Arthur was a widower who liked to run the social side of the White House himself. Grover Cleveland entered the White House as a bachelor, and then became the first President to be married within its walls.

Her name was Frances Folsom. Beautiful, well-dressed, well-educated, modest and twenty-two years old, she seemed the answer to the society pages' perpetual need for a Fairy Queen. When the story of the impending marriage leaked out, the American press converged on the White House. At first it seemed that Cleveland could not have made a better choice. He was hardly Prince Charming—not at three hundred pounds, anyway. He had been something of a drinker, a smoker, and there had been rumors about him and the ladies. His image would be polished by his bride-to-be.

The couple exasperated the press. They wanted privacy. Cleveland called the journalists "the ghouls." After a quiet ceremony in the Blue Room, bride and groom waited until dark and slipped out a back door of the White House. The press pursued them to Maryland and set up telescopes and field glasses. The local police beat the bushes and flushed the reporters to a greater distance.

America loved its new First Lady; Washington Society wanted to claim her; and the press wanted to tell all. For one so young, she was levelheaded and utterly resistant to Queen fever. She tried to relieve the pressure by

Julia Grant

Lucy Hayes

183

Julia Dent Grant found the White House "a bright and beautiful dream."

Lucy Ware Webb Hayes abolished alcohol in the White House and was nicknamed "Lemonade Lucy."

Frances Cleveland

Caroline Harrison

Frances Folsom Cleveland was so popular that the Marines had to protect her from admirers.

Caroline Lavinia Scott Harrison was a grandmother interested in flower arrangements, the Daughters of the American Revolution, and a larger White House.

184

instituting noon receptions a few times a week, but ladies screamed and fainted, and the Marines had to take the situation in hand. She only attracted minor mutterings: the National Woman's Temperance Convention was held in Washington and earnestly requested young women to "refrain from wearing the décolleté style of dress because it is immodest and fraught with dangerous and immoral influences." The notice was sent by telegram to the White House. There is no record of acknowledgment. Nor were the First Lady's dresses altered.

Frances Cleveland did the best she could. She only flared up once, in the early days. Colonel Lamont, Cleveland's secretary, asked one of the more sensible reporters for a means of defending against an advertisement that was typical of those then flooding the country.

"Many have been the remarks about the complexion of the First Lady. . . . The secret of her beautiful complexion has at last been given to the wife of a General famous during the late War. It is simply the use of arsenic, which can safely be taken and which can be procured from the New York doctor whose name is signed to this advertisement."

The only possible defense was silence.

The more modest, sensible, and domestic she seemed, the more the country loved her, and the more the press wanted her. She met five thousand people at a reception and she produced "five thousand smiles and no two alike." Washington high life was stratospheric. It became the rage to give entertainments of special colors: "pink teas, orange receptions, and blue and purple affairs." Frances Cleveland avoided the excesses. Her only innovation was a new style of wearing her hair in a low knot on the nape of the neck. "Seven out of every ten women in Washington copied her and the style has been adopted throughout the country."

Her popularity was a leading factor in Cleveland's defeat by Benjamin Harrison. Harrison's friends put out the story that the President was a drunk who beat his wife and turned her out of the White House. It was cleverly timed so that the denial never caught up with the story. The denial was written by Mrs Cleveland herself. "I can wish the women of our country no greater blessing than that their homes and lives may be as happy, and their husbands may be as kind, attentive, considerate, and affectionate as mine."

Though Grover Cleveland had become immensely popular, this low canard and his low tariff policies defeated him. Ironically it was said that "Grover Cleveland is the most popular person today in the United States—with the exception of Mrs Cleveland."

185

One stands in awe of her, even at this distance. In addition to steadiness and beauty, she had the minor ability to read the future clearly. On leaving the White House she turned to the Chief of the White House staff and said, "I want to find everything just as it is now when we come back again. We are coming back just four years from today."

She was right.

Mrs Harrison was domestic and interested in flowers; Mrs Cleveland returned and was domestic and interested in babies; Mrs McKinley was domestic and an invalid. The relationship between White House wives and press had calmed. Somewhere between Mary Lincoln and the turn of the century an unspoken protocol between the White House wives and the press had been worked out. The women no longer pretended to be imperiously regal, but were content with being eminently respectable. The breed of lady journalists who had risen with the Civil War and Reconstruction aged away, and their passions were taken up by the suffrage movement.

Washington's Society still yearned for a Leader, and a Central Authority. The White House ladies were never again to make the effort. Others took their place.

Washington's Society had always differed from New York, Boston, and Philadelphia Society. Outside the nation's capital, Society could be entered by family or fortune. "Once admitted, always accepted" was the rule of the Grand Families. Custom and tradition centralized the authority. But in Washington, names could be dropped every four years. An election meant an emendation of the Social lists.

It was a chilling bath for unwary wives of statesmen and politicians. In a diary of the wife of a newly appointed Cabinet minister there reads the notation:

"I am finally realized. The men listen; the women are awed . . ." Four years later she writes: "Where are my friends?"

The people proposed and the people disposed. For this reason the Grand Families outside the capital have always considered Washington Society unstable and parvenu. In his short story "Pandora," Henry James disguises Henry Adams who says, "Let us be vulgar and have some fun. Let us invite the President." Adams in his novel "Democracy" has a leading character say, "I wish we had never come to Washington. New York is so much nicer and the people there are much more amusing; they dance ever so much better and send one flowers all the time, and then they never talk about first principles."

At the worst, temporary power leads to nervousness. One wants to know as quickly as possible where one stands. D. B. Randolph Keim published at the turn of the century his *Handbook of Official and Social Etiquette and Public Ceremonials at Washington* which dissected the social world of Washington in 230 pages. There were three main court circles: the Official Class including the President and his important employees; the Quasi-official Class, or the Diplomatic Corps; and the Non-official Class. In the Official Class there were twenty-five ranks. It was confusing even in those days.

Whatever the listing, it always causes more dissent than admiration. When Edith Roosevelt gave a diplomatic dinner, she invited Admiral George Dewey, the recently returned hero of Manila. Dewey thought that White House protocol ought to rank him above the ministers and below the ambassadors. In naval tradition the admiral rated a seventeen-gun salute which was "greater by two than a Foreign Minister," and his cannons ought to be heard at the White House. Mrs Roosevelt did not surrender.

The same administration saw the first social secretary assigned to a First Lady, adding another layer of insulation. Isabelle Hagner was a power to be respected: "She has merely to raise her finger to Charles the footman, and he is at her elbow; to Mr. Stone, the head usher (formerly a Pullman car conductor), she has only to impart an order and it is obeyed. She is pointed out as the one woman in all Washington who has absolute freedom in the White House."

Edith Roosevelt liked raising flowers and disliked shaking hands. Just before each reception she saw that her guests were presented with flowers whose colors corresponded to the gowns. "Handshaking is thus obviated to a great extent," reported the press.

The marriage of Alice Roosevelt, Teddy's daughter, to Congressman Nicholas Longworth of Cincinnati was the leading social flurry of the time.

The Empress of China, the President of France, the King of Italy, the Emperor of Japan, the Pope, and the King of Spain sent gifts in the name of their country. Edward VII of England sent nothing; a year earlier Alice had wanted to attend his coronation and because of a squabble as to rank she was prohibited from going.

She was her father's daughter. On her wedding day she had trouble cutting the heavily glazed cake. The New York *Herald* reporter said:

"The cutting proceeded much too slowly for a young woman of her impulsive disposition, and gaily turning to Major McCawley, she cried out, 'Oh, Major, let me have your sword to cut the cake with.'

"The Major, who is too *au fait* to be surprised at anything, promptly drew his sword and extended the hilt to her. It happened to be a sabre and admirably adapted to the purpose, and when Mrs. Longworth brandished it

Edith Roosevelt

Helen Taft

188

Edith Kermit Carow Roosevelt was not impressed by Admiral Dewey. Helen Herron Taft practiced music openly and politics covertly.

Theodore Roosevelt's daughter, Alice, as a debutante in the White House.

aloft and began slashing the cake with it, the slices fell right and left, and great was the scramble among her friends for it. It melted away like snow under a hot sun, and within marvelously few minutes after the first stroke of Major McCawley's sabre, not a crumb of it was to be had."

Theodore Roosevelt had the problem of choosing his successor. He declined a third time, but knew the country would accept whatever candidate he chose. He wavered between Charles Evans Hughes and William Howard Taft. TR delighted in teasing the two men. There is a revealing anecdote which introduces Helen Herron Taft. President Roosevelt announced over brandy that he was "the seventh son of a seventh daughter." He saw something hanging over Taft's head. Was it the Presidency or the Chief Justiceship?

"Make it the Chief Justiceship," pleaded Taft.

"Make it the Presidency," said Mrs Taft.

Mrs Taft had her way. Theodore Roosevelt nodded, and the new President was all but elected.

Helen Taft practiced music openly and politics covertly. She had spent a great deal of time in the White House during Hayes' presidency. Her father had been Hayes' law partner and she was backstage during her husband's campaign. She thought that a woman should not attract attention to herself as a politician. She wrote:

"I am not trying to pose as a woman endowed with an especial comprehension of such problems as men alone have been trained to deal with . . ."

But her husband was more honest. He is quoted as saying:

"If I were presiding in the Supreme Court . . . I should feel entirely at home. However, as my wife is the politician and she will be able to meet all these issues, perhaps we can keep a stiff upper lip . . ."

An old theme in the history of the wives of the White House was again emerging. The wives of three successive Presidents—Taft, Wilson, and Harding—would exert a strong political influence on the White House. This tendency had begun a long time before, but the issue would soon come to a boil-over point. The issue was not so much the wife's influence on the husband's decisions: it was that the women stayed in the President's shadow, and publicly denied their private influence.

With Helen Taft, the situation was not yet dangerous. She traveled a great deal with her husband, and was responsible for importing the Japanese cherry

Ellen Wilson

Edith Wilson

Ellen Wilson died a year after her husband became President.

Edith Bolling Galt Wilson fought for her husband's political life.

191

trees to Washington. A solid, matronly type from Cincinnati, she celebrated her silver anniversary in the White House.

Her successor was the first Mrs Wilson. Thematically, she was a continuation of the eminently respectable First Ladies.

She had to be; her husband had trouble with women. Political trouble, to begin with. The suffragettes picketed the White House continuously, and sent imploring notes to Mrs Wilson to join their cause. Mrs Wilson had a more difficult problem with less militant women. Some men pay court by flexing their muscles; Woodrow Wilson flexed his intellect. The more beautiful his audience, the more his mind rippled. He would lead some belle into a cozy corner of the White House, and talk brilliantly, on and on.

He not only talked, he wrote letters.

If Mrs Wilson felt the serpent, she neither let her jealousy be shown nor confided to anyone.

She died, just as World War I broke out.

The private lives of Presidents are taboo, and for a good reason. A President touches his people and history by the acts he accomplishes and by nothing else. His personal motivations; the insurrections of his mind as he comes up to a decision; these properly should be kept dark and unrecorded. That Wilson had to talk to confidantes; that he had to talk to a woman; none of this diminishes the quality of his acts or his place in the American experience.

He fell in love again, too quickly for mores. She was Edith Bolling Galt, a Washington widow. He wanted to marry her before he announced for reelection. To Wilson's advisers, it was a rash move. Colonel House, Wilson's gray eminence, and William Gibbs McAdoo, his son-in-law, felt an early announcement would be politically disastrous. They tried to block the engagement.

Wilson had written letters to Mrs Mary Hulbert Peck—about two hundred of them. Scholars who have read the letters say there was nothing compromising in them, but obviously Wilson thought there was. McAdoo and House let Wilson know that if he announced his engagement to Mrs Galt the letters would be published by Mrs Peck. Wilson took to his bed. In the light of modern medicine, this may have been the precursor stroke that usually precedes the thrombosis from which he later died.

Mrs Galt came to his bedside. The conversation was not recorded, except by Mrs Galt who wrote that their conversation went on for hours. On October 7, 1915, they publicly announced their engagement. Neither Mrs Peck nor the country had anything evil to say. Only the President bore the scars.

The consequence of the drama was that Edith Galt Wilson was continuously at her husband's side, not only during the inevitable ceremonials, but in the President's planning of America's participation in World War I. During the war she was his confidential secretary and closest adviser. She decoded some of his personal cables and coded others. He spiraled deeper and deeper into the work of the Presidency, and only his new wife could bring him to necessary diversions and relaxations.

When the Allies were victorious, the Wilsons went abroad. His ideas had touched the citizenry of Europe in a way that no American had done since the Revolution. The Peace of Versailles was not written by him. He was forced to compromise. He thought each compromise would be regained when the League of Nations came into being.

The League never included the United States. When it became apparent that the Senate would refuse to ratify either the Peace Treaty or America's entrance into the League, the Wilsons took their case to the American people. The fever of disenchantment had touched America. The President could not treat it with the same brave rhetoric which had put America into the war. He collapsed again.

Then came one of the most mysterious eras in the history of the wives of the White House. The rumor was that Mrs Wilson was the acting head of the United States, and that the President was incapacitated. If he were truly incapable, the Constitution provides that he be replaced. A committee headed by Senator Albert Fall, made a supposedly friendly call on Mr Wilson and found him in the Lincoln bed. His wife was seated at his side, equipped with paper and pencil.

Senator Fall said to her: "You seem to be very much engaged, madam."

Mrs Wilson answered: "Yes, I thought it wise to record this interview so there may be no misunderstandings or misstatements made."

Fall remarked to the President: "We have all been praying for you."

Wilson answered: "Which way, Senator?"

The period is sometimes called "the Mrs Wilson Regency."

There seems little doubt that she was the surrogate President. Mrs Wilson says that she decided only which matters the President should see, and which were to be kept from him. She offered Cabinet posts, "in the name of her husband, of course."

The documentation of her regency is sparse. Now that she is dead, perhaps more will be said. She was the first First Lady to come out of the White House and do political battle, without hiding fully behind her husband. Yet she did not announce herself as a public figure.

The Hardings entered the White House at the beginning of "The Era of Wonderful Nonsense," the 1920s. The stories of the scandals and of the

Presidency are documented more fully elsewhere, but Florence Harding belonged to a school of White House wives that cut across chronology. The closest parallel to her was Eliza Johnson who taught an illiterate tailor how to read and write after their marriage. Mrs Harding taught politics to her husband.

Warren Gamaliel Harding was her second husband. Her first marriage had ended in divorce, and her father, a rich Ohio banker, disapproved of her marriage to a man some six years her junior. She broke with her father and married a man who would have been content to be a small-town editor for the rest of his life.

She has been described as "shrewd and keen, with the mind of a man," but like Mrs Wilson before her, no one was neutral about her influence on her husband. She saw early that her husband looked like the very model of a government official, and she was keen enough to see that Ohio was becoming a pivotal state in American politics. Harding served in the Senate, and Mrs Harding learned about Washington politics.

For the public record, she tried to stay in the background. Publicly, she said, "Don't ask him to run," but Harry Daugherty, who came out of a smoke-filled room with Harding's nomination, all but took orders from Mrs Harding. America elected a man who said he "wasn't sure he wanted to be President."

As a White House hostess, Mrs Harding re-established the social functions which had been eliminated by the war and the Wilsons. Prohibition was enforced—but not upstairs, where the President poured liquor for "the Ohio Gang." There is no doubt that Mrs Harding had more than a hand in appointments up to the Cabinet level. When Harry Daugherty was being considered as Attorney General, Alice Roosevelt Longworth came to her and the President and implored them to reconsider. Organized labor and the Bar Association were horrified at their choice, but Daugherty got the job.

Her friends might be rewarded, but the Vice President and his wife were not in the inner group. Early in the Harding administration a bill came up to provide the Vice President with a fine home in Washington. She saw to it that the bill was killed: "I just couldn't have people like those Coolidges living in that beautiful house."

She probably would have made a better President than her husband. She tried to guide him but he was not his own man. Mrs Harding fell ill during the second year, and on her convalescence found the situation out of control. The change in public sentiment was extreme. Gossip concerning the President's public and private life preceded the evidence. Mrs Harding began a personal fight to clear her husband, but she was not powerful enough to turn the current.

Mrs Kennedy's Green Room. The sofa belonged to Daniel Webster. All the furniture dates from the Federal period, about 1800. The pictures have been changed since the broadcast.

The scandals killed him. The Hardings had gone on a visit to Alaska and then returned to San Francisco. The President collapsed while Mrs Harding ostensibly was reading an extremely favorable magazine article praising him. In the middle of "A Calm View of a Calm Man" he had a stroke and died.

Once he was dead, the scandals broke and the whispering was printed. Nan Britton wrote a book intimating that President Harding had fathered her illegitimate child. The climax of the scandals was the prison sentence given to Secretary of Interior Albert Fall (the same man who had inquired so carefully after Wilson's health). In prison one Gaston Means, who had used the Bureau of Investigation for his own purposes, wrote a book claiming that Mrs Harding had poisoned her husband.

Harding's coffin lay in state in the East Room. Mrs Harding talked to the dead President for hours. She must have said a great deal. There were people in the room, but her only recorded remark is: "No one can hurt you now, Warren."

She died a few months later. Florence Harding was the last President's wife to try to do political battle hidden completely behind her husband. Mrs Franklin Roosevelt would revive the tradition of a woman in politics, but she would do it as a public figure in her own right.

Calvin Coolidge always claimed that he had been chosen by the Republican convention as a reaction to Warren Harding. He was an astringent relief after the floridity of Harding: a dry New Englander, obviously as honest as Vermont granite; sworn into the Presidency by his father in a scene lit by a kerosene lantern.

Mrs Coolidge was an equal reaction to Mrs Harding. She shunned publicity and knew nothing about politics. "I am rather proud of the fact that after nearly a quarter of a century of marriage my husband feels free to make his decisions and act on them without consulting me." Mrs Coolidge dressed well, was unassuming, and saw her role as a kind of safety valve for her husband. That Silent Cal was capable of temper is evident in her statement: "I have scant patience with the man of whom his wife says 'He never gave me a cross word in his life.' If a man amounts to much in this world, he must encounter many annoyances whose number mounts as his effectiveness increases. Inevitably comes a point beyond which human endurance breaks down, and an explosion is bound to follow."

Calvin Coolidge's explosions were private and unrecorded. His public style was cool and terse. He gave up the Presidency in ten words: "I do not choose to run in 1928."

Herbert and Lou Hoover were wealthy, philanthropic, and ended regionalism as a leading force in choosing a President. Mrs Hoover was a world-

Florence Harding

Grace Coolidge

Florence Kling Harding taught politics to her husband.

Grace Anna Goodhue Coolidge shunned publicity and cared little about politics.

Lou Henry Hoover spoke five languages, was President of the Girl Scouts of America, and set the best table in White House history.

Lou Hoover

traveler. Her husband proposed to her by cable from London and she replied from California in one word; "Yes." She followed him to China, was in Tientsin, and traveled through Europe with him during the war. She spoke five languages, read books on economics and sociology before going to bed, presided over luncheons for as many as 1800 guests and was an active president of the Girl Scouts. If this were not enough, she received delegations, directed assemblies, appeared at college commencements, christened new ships, built log cabins, and raised two sons. She had all the virtues that should have attracted public attention, including modesty. They were all hidden behind the Depression and she has never received the accolade due her. She is remembered by Washington as the woman who set the best table in White House history.

Eleanor Roosevelt paid no attention to food. Her eldest son has written: "She has no appreciation for fine food. Victuals to her are something to inject into the body as fuel to keep it going, much as a motorist pours gasoline into an auto tank." According to Robert Sherwood, the White House served salads "which resembled the productions one finds in the flossier type of tea shoppe." Franklin Roosevelt sent sad notes to his wife recalling "I got sick of chicken because I got it at least six times a week. I am getting to the point where my stomach positively rebels and this does not help my relations with foreign powers. I bit two of them today."

Nor did Mrs Roosevelt pay much attention to physical aspects of the White House. She is supposed to have made a tour of the mansion shortly after her arrival and instructed the ushers to get all the antiques on the second floor out of sight. They seemed too frail for an energetic family like the Roosevelts. She liked to conduct tours personally, and once led a group of lobstermen directly into the family quarters, which had been sanctimoniously private until then. She brought them in and out of a bedroom quickly—her daughter Anna was asleep on the bed.

During the four terms of her stay in the White House, there were thirteen grandchildren dashing in and out of the building and playing in the corridors. The building was far too small. Although the Roosevelts stayed longer in the White House than any presidential family in American history, the mansion was never considered more than a temporary rental. Home was Hyde Park, the patrician estate in New York. The Roosevelts were so patrician and so democratic that they had no fear of royalty. Mrs Roosevelt served the King and Queen of England a plate of hotdogs, a butler tripped and dropped a tray of martinis before their Majesties—and Mrs Roosevelt wrote a column about it.

Eleanor Roosevelt made over the rules. She did not break them all, but

197

Anna Eleanor Roosevelt had little interest in food but paid a great deal of attention to international affairs.

White House protocol was not made for a woman like her. She entered politics, not behind the President, but joyously in front of him. She told the nation that she tried to influence the political decisions of her husband. It seems clear now that President Roosevelt grew progressively more conservative as his terms went on, while his wife became more liberal. As early as 1938, when the Spanish Civil War was going on and some refugees were trapped in Madrid, she cabled FDR: ARE YOU OR THE STATE DEPARTMENT DOING ANYTHING.

She did not hesitate to criticize the political actions and information of her husband, the President of the United States. Just before World War II:

"What you told me on scrap iron being only a small amount was incorrect and [The State Department's] whole attitude seems to me weak. We help China with one hand and we appease and help Japan with the other. Why can't we decide what is right and do it?"

Undoubtedly Mrs Roosevelt was the overwhelming reason Henry A. Wallace was chosen as the candidate for Vice President by the Democratic Convention of 1940. A lesser woman might have stumbled more often, but Eleanor Roosevelt became legendary. Year after year young American women voted her as the woman they most admired in American life, and newspapers who were in political opposition to her husband carried Mrs Roosevelt's column "My Day."

The social life of the White House was hot and turbulent. Aside from the official functions of the office, the ceremonial dinners and the diplomatic receptions, Mrs Roosevelt used social functions in the President's house for political purposes. She once managed two teas simultaneously: she had representatives of capital in the Red Room, representatives of labor in the Green Room, and she opened the connecting doors to the Blue Room.

To some degree she had been thrust into this kind of life by her husband's illness. She was "the eyes and ears" of a man in a wheelchair. But the handicaps of her own life had given her a will of her own. Although reared in fashionable elegance and educated in the best schools of America and Europe, she had been a shy, timid girl. Her mother-in-law dominated the first few years of her marriage. By strength of will, Eleanor Roosevelt decided to devote her life to her family and to public service. For a woman who wrote notes about major problems in foreign affairs, the daily details of raising a family or keeping the White House were only problems in logistics. She had her share of maternal and grandmaternal anxieties: the Roosevelt clan always had a mind of its own. She worried about FDR's third term and opposed it. She was mother, wife, politician, stateswoman, journalist, and First Lady—all at once, and often all at the same time.

When she left the White House an usher remarked: "This place needs a rest."

Bess Truman reacted to Eleanor Roosevelt as Elizabeth Monroe had reacted to Dolley Madison. Both later First Ladies withdrew from active public life. Mrs Truman let it be known that she didn't want to live in the White House, and her appearances would be only ceremonial, and only as necessary. Whereas Mrs Roosevelt had her own press conferences in what was then the Monroe Room, Mrs Truman would be heard only through the voice of her private secretary. Margaret Truman, her daughter, was her surrogate. Mrs Truman had "no comment" to make, and Americans respected her privacy as much as they had respected Mrs Roosevelt's public life. She succeeded mightily in her quest for anonymity. There have been several books covering the Truman era in the White House. All contain the same sentence, or a slight variation of it: "Mrs Truman chose plum for her bedroom." Obviously the door was closed to court reporters.

Mamie Eisenhower left it closed. Her husband won the presidency twice, and was the most popular American figure since the early days of Franklin Roosevelt. Mrs Eisenhower went through the necessary ceremonials, but it seemed clear that after so many years as an Army wife, she was looking more toward a farm at Gettysburg than to the stay at the White House. Like Mrs Truman she gave no speeches, expressed no political opinions, and remained out of public reach.

It is too early to make judgments about Mrs Kennedy's role in the White House. Her biography gives some clues: she was born July 28, 1929, in Southampton, New York. She attended a private school in Farmington, Connecticut, and Vassar College. She studied the history of art at the Sorbonne, Paris. She graduated from George Washington University in 1951, studying American history. In 1952 she served on the staff of the Washington *Times-Herald*. She speaks French, Spanish, and Italian. She married John F. Kennedy at Newport, September 12, 1953. She has two children: Caroline, born in 1957, and John F. Jr., born in 1960.

It is tempting to say that she seems to be one of the brilliant exceptions in the history of the wives who have lived in the White House. Her interest in the arts recalls a half-dozen of her predecessors, but there has probably never been so strong an attempt to reward the intellectual community of America by Presidential recognition as the effort she is now making. Her plans to restore the White House are not revolutionary; the reader will recognize that other First Ladies have restored the Executive Mansion. Again, her concentra-

Elizabeth Truman

Mamie Eisenhower

Elizabeth Virginia Wallace Truman shunned publicity and attended ceremonials only when necessary.

Mamie Geneva Doud Eisenhower gave no speeches, expressed no political opinions, and remained out of public reach.

tion and scholarship seem more intense than anyone who has preceded her. Her popularity with the American public echoes the acclaim given to other First Ladies. Although her interest in politics is apparent, it is by no means a fundamental drive. Mrs Kennedy has pointedly avoided the political as have the majority of President's wives. Finally, her insistence on privacy and domesticity is the oldest theme in the White House.

She is the youngest First Lady of this century and the third youngest wife of a President to live in the White House. Her beauty and youth are novelties for this century. But it is best not to try to make a summation. Mrs Kennedy can speak for herself, and America will judge for itself. It seems unlikely that the judgment will be unfavorable.

THE SECOND FLOOR

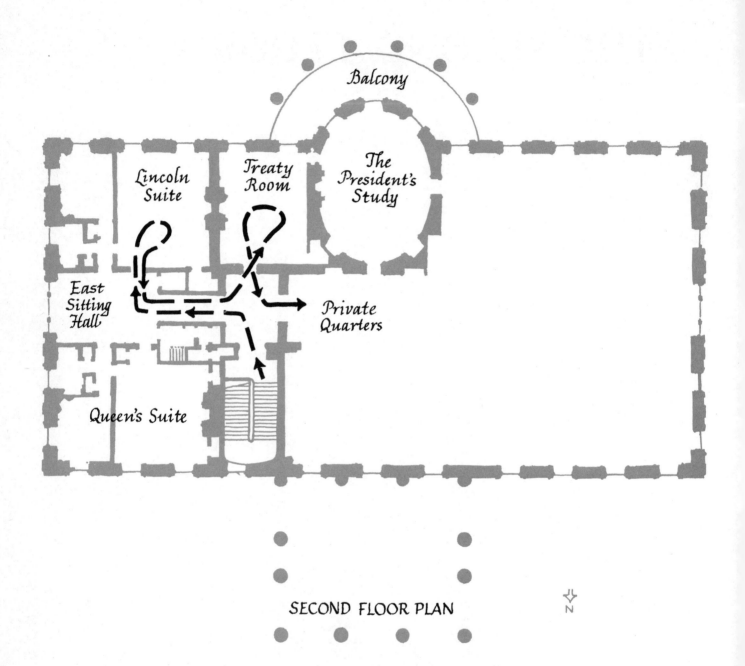

Balcony

Lincoln Suite

Treaty Room

The President's Study

East Sitting Hall

Private Quarters

Queen's Suite

SECOND FLOOR PLAN

N

The broken line indicates the path of Mrs Kennedy during the television program.

MRS KENNEDY showed only two of the fifteen or more rooms which make up the second floor. The privacy of the family quarters was respected. The Lincoln and Treaty Rooms are on the east side of the second floor in an area where guests of state are lodged. Unlike the ground and first floor, the main corridor on the second floor is interrupted by two pairs of sliding doors which divide this part of the White House into a series of apartments. Thus there are three interrupted segments of corridor which have been treated as rooms. The whole floor must be seen as a grouping of suites.

The records concerning the evolution of the rooms are far less exact than on the floor below. The present arrangement dates from the 1952 renovation. There is a two-room suite on the northeast side of the building sometimes called the Rose Suite, or the Queen's Suite. At least four Queens have occupied it during their visits to the United States. The Lincoln Room adjoins a small dressing room; together the two compose the Lincoln Suite. Between the Lincoln Suite and the Rose Suite is a section of corridor which has been furnished as a room, and is called the East Sitting Hall. This whole area is elevated a few feet in order that the ceiling of the East Room, one floor below, be of sufficient height. Until Franklin Roosevelt's administration, there were a few steps between the east section and the balance of the second floor, but in FDR's day a ramp was installed for his wheelchair.

The room which Mrs Kennedy is furnishing as the Treaty Room was once called the Monroe Room. Between it and the President's study is a door which has been alternatively sealed up or left open. Until 1902, the eastern area of the second floor was the office section.

The oval room on the second floor is traditionally the President's study, although it has been used as a reception room, a drawing room, and a music room. The furnishings of this room have varied widely, from formal crimsons and mahogany to chintzes. Mrs Taft placed teakwood furniture and Oriental screens reminiscent of the Philippines in this room. Franklin Roosevelt returned the room to a President's study in 1933. Mrs Kennedy's personal furniture has been placed in this room. Her choice centers on authentic Louis XVI pieces, around which she has gathered a harmonious group of objects.

The fact that Mrs Kennedy's personal choice of furniture is not the same as the periods in which she has chosen to decorate the balance of the White

205

House is another example of the distinction between the private and public areas of the President's house. The public rooms are part of the American heritage: the President's personal furniture is his own affair, for no man will stay in the White House for more than eight years.

It has been a long diversion since Mrs Kennedy left the first floor.

The Second Floor

One of the offices on the second floor, about 1890. The makeshift telephone wires and the improvised lighting arrangements show the clutter which Theodore Roosevelt ordered out of the building. This room is just a few feet from the private quarters of the President's family.

The old second floor map room is now part of the Lincoln Suite. This photograph shows naval positions during the Spanish-American War.

The Lincoln Room when it was a President's study.

The desk has a long history. It was made from the timbers of a British man-of-war, HMS *Resolute,* when the ship was broken up. Queen Victoria had the desk made and sent "to the President of the United States as a memorial of . . . loving kindness."

208

The desk was used by many Presidents until Franklin Roosevelt put it in storage. After the 1952 restoration, it was placed on the ground floor. Mrs Kennedy found it hidden under a green cloth. President Kennedy now uses it in his office in the Executive Wing.

. . . and some detective work

The Lincoln Room, as Mrs Kennedy enters from the sitting room in the East Hall. The Lincoln bed is in the foreground. The chair next to the bureau was in this room when President Lincoln used it as his Cabinet Room.

(Mrs Kennedy and Mr Collingwood enter the Lincoln Room)

MR COLLINGWOOD

Mrs Kennedy, do you spend a great deal of time in the Lincoln Room?

MRS KENNEDY

We did in the beginning. It was where we lived when we first came here when our rooms at the other end of the hall were being painted. I loved living in this room. It's on the sunny side of the house and one of Andrew Jackson's magnolia trees is right outside the window.

MR COLLINGWOOD

It's a nice room. Was this a bedroom during Lincoln's time?

MRS KENNEDY

No, it was Lincoln's Cabinet Room. It was President Truman—who's such a scholar of American history—who turned it into a shrine to Lincoln and took the Lincoln furniture that had been all over the house and put it in this room.

MR COLLINGWOOD

Are all the pieces from Lincoln's time?

MRS KENNEDY

Yes they are. The most famous one, of course, is the Lincoln bed. Every President seemed to love it. Theodore Roosevelt slept in it. So did Calvin Coolidge. It's probably the most famous piece of furniture in the White House. It was bought by Mrs Lincoln along with the dressing bureaus and chair and this table. She bought a lot of furniture for this house. She made her husband

210

The chair in the previous photograph is the same as the one in the right foreground of this painting. Francis B. Carpenter, a New York artist, painted Lincoln and his Cabinet at the first reading of the Emancipation Proclamation, which was signed in this room. Once, when a visitor came for a private talk with Lincoln and hesitated to speak in Carpenter's presence, Lincoln said: "Oh, you need not mind him; he is but a painter." Carpenter ignored the quarrels and ambitions of Lincoln's Cabinet and painted the men as calm and benevolent advisors to the President.

211

rather cross because he thought she spent too much money. This table was also loved by Mrs Theodore Roosevelt. She wrote to McKim, Mead & White and told them to be sure and stain the furniture in the rest of her bedroom the same color as this table.

MR COLLINGWOOD

It's quite a table. Is that all carving?

MRS KENNEDY

Yes it is—fantastic Victorian carving. And on the table is the Gettysburg Address. This is probably the greatest treasure in the room because it's one of only five copies written in his own hand. Yellow paper has been kept over it so it won't fade. This is also the room where Lincoln signed the Emancipation Proclamation.

MR COLLINGWOOD

On the desk?

MRS KENNEDY

No, not on that desk. That desk was in the Soldiers' Home where he used to go as sort of a summer retreat in Washington or to telegraph. And this sofa and the two chairs were brought here through the efforts of President Truman.

MR COLLINGWOOD

Hasn't all sorts of detective work gone into finding these pieces and identifying them?

MRS KENNEDY

Yes, these two chairs are an example of that. We found one at Fort Washington, which is the storehouse; so battered, all the

The chair next to the bed was discovered by Mrs Kennedy and her aides in the government storehouse at Fort Washington. Its duplicate was discovered later, and a donor sent just enough Victorian green and yellow velvet to cover the two chairs.

The Lincoln Bed is the most famous object in the White House. It is nine feet long and made of solid rosewood.

stuffing coming out. But we just thought it looked of the Lincoln period so we dragged it home. And we found from an engraving that it was. And then out of the blue a Mrs Millard Black of Arlington sent us its exact pair. And then a Mrs Burton Cohen from New Jersey sent us some Victorian green and yellow Morris velvet and it was just enough to cover the two chairs. So here they are, Lincoln's chairs.

MR COLLINGWOOD

Is that dressing bureau with the mirror part of the original Lincoln furniture because it's a marvelously masculine piece?

MRS KENNEDY

Yes. That was one of the things that Mrs Lincoln bought. Almost everything in this room is—except that mirror which was bought about 1870 and I think it's been all over the house. The last we know of it was that it was in the Blue Room over the Monroe pier table in McKinley's time.

MR COLLINGWOOD

What's the picture of Andrew Jackson doing in the Lincoln Room?

MRS KENNEDY

Oh well, you see, Lincoln loved Andrew Jackson and from an old engraving we found that when this was his Cabinet Room he had that picture hanging in it. So we took the picture, which was downstairs, and put it in the same place that he had it. And the two chairs under it were also bought in the time of Jackson but Lincoln used them as his cabinet chairs. There are only four left now but because this was his cabinet room we keep the chairs here.

During Benjamin Harrison's administration, the Lincoln Bed was still canopied. The original description of the bed was made in 1862: "Twenty feet above the floor overspreading the whole, is a magnificent canopy . . . being in the form of a crown . . . The drapery is a rich purple satin print and otherwise ornamented with the finest gold lace. The carved work is adorned with gold gilt."

Well, if this was his Cabinet Room, Mrs Kennedy, where was his office?

His office was next door. In his day you could walk through to it, without coming out in the hall, because the hall was always crowded with office seekers. They really plagued him and to escape them, he would just slip through the door.

So this whole wing was an office wing for a long time in the White House?

Yes, until Theodore Roosevelt built the office buildings in 1902.

(*They exit Lincoln Room*)

The Lincoln Room is the only room in the White House devoted to a single President. In a sense, it is the precursor of all Mrs Kennedy's work. It has already been noted that sometime in the 1920s the history of American furniture began to have something more than an academic and parochial appeal. Mrs Coolidge and Mrs Hoover collected artifacts which had relationships with earlier Presidents. The Lincoln furnishings were the first objects of interest. The work continued sporadically through the next three administrations.

A number of Lincoln artifacts came from Mr John Witt, 15 Dorset Square, London. All pieces had to be authenticated, photographed, repaired, re-upholstered, shipped and delivered. The process took over two years. A London firm which appraised the gifts noted they were clearly "Victorian furniture such as used daily in the homes of middle classes [showing] strong influence of German and Austrian designed furniture."

President Truman began the necessary arrangements to acquire the pieces, but they were not placed in the Lincoln Room until President Eisenhower's era. Both Presidents took a keen interest in the acquisitions.

The authentication of Lincoln furniture is a complicated task worthy of a small detour. As the reader can imagine, if all the supposed Lincoln furniture in the country were to be brought together, a hundred warehouses would be filled to capacity. Aside from simple fraud as practiced on the

The Second Floor

216

The elaborately carved Victorian table in the Lincoln Room is part of the furnishings purchased by Mary Lincoln. Between the table legs is a carved bird's nest, complete with eggs.

Atop the table is the Gettysburg Address. President Lincoln wrote and signed this copy on lined paper for a Civil War charity sale. This is one of five copies made by the President.

217

periphery of the world of antiques, the Lincoln legend has contributed to the volume of supposed Lincoln furniture. The totally false story that Mary Lincoln sold White House furniture is the basis on which many people have believed that they owned original Lincoln pieces. A good example is given by the Lincoln chairs which Mrs Kennedy discussed in the Red Room. They are not in the Lincoln Room for good reason:

In 1961 Mrs Edythe McGinnis, a White House employee working in the gift-receiving room, thought she might have two chairs which belonged to Lincoln. She brought one to the White House curator who promptly recognized it as a fine example of chairs belonging to the period 1830–50. Mrs McGinnis' family presumed the pieces were bought in a sale of White House furniture held several weeks after Lincoln's assassination. She remembered that the original upholstery was mohair, and that a large swatch of the material was mounted for some twenty-five years on the wall of the Oldest Inhabitants Club in Washington. Edythe McGinnis' grandfather had bought six or seven chairs. Experts now believe the pieces had been purchased for the White House much earlier than Lincoln's tenancy. Nevertheless, it was established that the two chairs had been in the mansion, and they were gratefully accepted. They are more likely from the time of Jackson, Van Buren, or Tyler. For this reason, they fit the style of the Red Room, and not the Lincoln Room. The story is typical: many antiques dating far earlier than Abraham Lincoln have been dubbed as "Lincoln pieces" as the Lincoln legends have grown—although the antiques have great value in their own right.

The center of the room is the Lincoln bed. It is the most famous piece of furniture in the White House. The legend is that the bed disappeared from the building and returned at an unspecified date. This story is incorrect: the bed has been in the mansion since Lincoln's time, and has never left the building.

The White House has records of almost every item purchased for decoration, dating from 1817. There are two bills from Lincoln's period for rosewood beds. One dates May 29, 1861; the other December 21, 1864. The 1861 invoice is the more likely bill of sale. It shows that the bed was purchased from William H. Sharyl, a Philadelphia furniture dealer. The document is on file at the National Capital Parks Service, and was found during the Truman administration. The National Archives shows a receipted bill for an invention new in Lincoln's time: "Pattent Spring Mattresses."

Many Presidents have used this bed. When Woodrow Wilson fell ill, visitors noted he was lying in the Lincoln bed. Mrs Coolidge crocheted a bedspread for it, one square per month for a period of two years. The bedspread was later

Lincoln used this desk when he went to the Soldier's Home near Washington to escape the crowds and the heat. The chair dates from the era of Andrew Jackson and is one of several types of straight back chairs used in Lincoln's Cabinet Room.

219

placed on a quilt, and the covering remained on the bed until Mrs Kennedy had it replaced. Mrs Roosevelt wrote that FDR's personal secretary, Louis Howe, slept in the bed. Margaret Truman invited some young ladies to spend the night with her, and although they tried to sleep in the bed, they found it too uncomfortable.

During Lincoln's time the room functioned as the Cabinet Room, and it was here that the Emancipation Proclamation was signed. A contemporary wrote:

"The roll containing the Emancipation Proclamation was taken to Mr Lincoln at noon by Secretary Seward and his son, Frederick. As it lay unrolled before him, Mr Lincoln took a pen, dipped it in ink, moved his hand to the place for the signature, held it a moment and dropped the pen. After a little hesitation he again took up the pen and went through the same movement as before.

"Mr Lincoln then turned to Mr Seward and said, 'I have been shaking hands since nine o'clock this morning and my right arm is almost paralyzed. If my name ever goes into history, it will be for this act and my whole soul is in it. If my hand trembles when I sign the Proclamation, all who examine the document will say: "He hesitated." '

"He then turned to the table, took up the pen again, and slowly, firmly wrote . . . '*Abraham Lincoln*.' "

Not all the objects in the room have so dignified a history. The portrait of Andrew Jackson is one of the oldest portraits in the house, and while Lincoln revered it, Theodore Roosevelt's son Quentin and his gang used it for target practice. They threw spitballs at the painting, and then arranged the spitballs in a decorative pattern on Andrew Jackson's forehead. Two were hung on his ear lobes as earrings. Theodore Roosevelt was furious. He made Quentin get out of bed to remove the paper, and held a kangaroo court for the rest of the gang, banishing them from the White House for seven days. TR noted, "They were four very sheepish small boys when I got through with them."

The whole episode echoes the pranks of Tad and Willie Lincoln. During the Civil War, when Lincoln's Cabinet met in this room, Tad Lincoln bombarded the meeting with his toy cannon. President Lincoln had to interrupt the discussion to restore peace. Tad Lincoln once stood behind his father when the President was reviewing Union troops and unfurled a Confederate flag. Lincoln pinned the boy's arms to his side and sent him back into the

White House.

The Treaty Room
... and the President

The Treaty Room, as Mrs Kennedy enters.

(They enter the Treaty Room)

Mrs Kennedy, I've often heard this room referred to as the Monroe Room. How did it get that name?

The Second Floor

It just came to be called that. It was Lincoln's office and Johnson's Cabinet Room. Then when it was used as an upstairs sitting room Mrs Hoover had three pieces of Monroe's furniture that were in his law office copied in the 1920s. But if you'll notice the inscription on this mantelpiece. It says, "This room was first used for meetings of the Cabinet during the administration of President Johnson, and continued to be so used until the year 1902. Here the treaty of peace with Spain was signed." You see, this was the Cabinet Room from Johnson to Theodore Roosevelt. Johnson thought there was bad luck associated with using Lincoln's Cabinet Room after his assassination. So he moved the Cabinet in here. This room is really a chamber of horrors now, but I thought it would be interesting for you to see what a room is like when we're starting to do it, because practically all the furniture in this room we found in storage so battered that there were cries of disbelief when I brought it home. But when this room is finished you'll see how impressive it will be. This sofa, for instance, was ordered by President Grant as was this table and chairs. There are a lot of them; we only have one left. And that mirror with the same shield. At Grant's Cabinet table there's a drawer for every member of the Cabinet. He would lock it up and take the key with him before the next meeting.

222

President Cleveland and his Cabinet meet in the Cabinet Room. This photograph shows some unusual details. The table belonged to General Grant. The spittoon in the left foreground and the empty, open light socket beside a rear portrait hardly fit the formal morning dress of the dignitaries.

223

MR COLLINGWOOD

What about the chairs around the Cabinet table, Mrs Kennedy?

MRS KENNEDY

Those were Grant's State Dining Room chairs. Then, from old engravings, we found that they were also used as Rutherford Hayes Private Dining Room chairs. We put them here. That desk is a gift to this room from Mrs Walter Gartner of South Wellfleet, Mass. It was Grant's wife's desk, Julia Grant. That's Grant's clock on it. This chair is interesting. It's the one that the Healy portrait of Lincoln in the dining room was painted on.

MR COLLINGWOOD

And you recognized it from the portrait?

MRS KENNEDY

Yes, we recognized it from the picture. This mirror which is broken in pieces, as you can see, we're going to put in the Red Room when we get it fixed. It's 1830; Andrew Jackson. It shouldn't be up here now but this is the room where all the clutter comes.

MR COLLINGWOOD

And on the walls there. I see you're trying out wallpaper. Is that it?

MRS KENNEDY

These are samples from documents of old wallpaper which were once in the White House. Sometimes we get a little scrap of it or we find it in a book. This piece isn't from the White House but this is the border of paper in the room where Lincoln died, across from Ford's Theatre. Everything else here has been in the White House at some time. And, the thing that we're going to do that

224

The Treaty Room.

    In the background, against the wall, is Julia Grant's clock. The chairs around the table belonged to Ulysses Grant and were used by Rutherford Hayes. The table was President Grant's cabinet desk.

will be interesting is so many treaties have been signed in this room—the Archives are going to give us copies of them all. We're going to frame them and have them all around the room so that you can really see this is such a historic room.

MR COLLINGWOOD

What are you going to do when you have it all finished?

MRS KENNEDY

Well I do think every room should have a purpose. It can still be a sitting room because that sofa, though you may not believe it, will look nice. But it will serve a definite purpose. My husband has so many meetings up here in this part of the house. All the men who wait to see him now sit in the hall with the baby carriages going by them. They can sit in here and talk while waiting for him.

MR COLLINGWOOD

Well, he's going to come in and see us in a few minutes.

(*They pause, awaiting President Kennedy*)

Andrew Jackson's mirror is on the floor behind Mrs Kennedy. Samples of wallpaper have been tacked up, and President Grant's sofa can be seen in black outline.   227

During the rehearsal period for the television program, Mrs Kennedy was asked why she was refurnishing the room. "It's really to get the Cabinet out of the living room," she said. During the broadcast she said the line quoted above, "All the men who wait to see him now sit in the hall with the baby carriages going by them."

All this is an example of living characteristics of the second floor. The state rooms on the floor below have had many changes in decoration, but few changes in purpose. A simple chronology of the new Treaty Room illustrates some functions of this single room on the second floor.

The Second Floor

In 1809 it was a large bedroom.

In 1825 John Quincy Adams made it a sitting room.

In 1849 it was a reception room adjoining the President's office.

In 1866 President Johnson made it his Cabinet Room.

In 1902 Theodore Roosevelt changed it into a study.

In 1929 Mrs Hoover made it a sitting room, and gave it the name "The Monroe Room."

In 1936 Mrs Roosevelt used it for her press conferences.

In 1945 Winston Churchill asked that it be changed into his personal map room.

In 1952 it was a sitting room.

In 1962 Mrs Kennedy made it the Treaty Room.

The room has had some ten different changes in purpose, and countless changes in décor. It is a leading example of the premise that the White House is neither a monument or a museum. Mrs Kennedy wants to turn it into a room which can be used for secret consultations, or for quickly called meetings during hours when the President does not wish to go to his official offices in the West Executive Wing. There is ample precedent for this change.

This was exactly the function of the room in the days of William Henry Harrison and John Tyler. Daniel Webster was Secretary of State to both Presidents. The room was closed and locked whenever a meeting was held. However, there was an obvious security leak; the deliberations of the Cabinet were reported in full in certain Washington newspapers, and all attempts to discover the source failed. One day Daniel Webster went into the oval room next door to find a book. He heard the voices of the members of the Cabinet leaking through the wall. Thereafter the adjoining room was emptied and locked before the President met with his Cabinet.

As for Mrs Kennedy's plans for décor, probably the most significant remark was made by an antique dealer who expressed himself in admiration of her courage: "She's trying to bring back the Victorian!" A cameraman called it "Technicians' Lounge furniture." Yet the basic pieces are sturdy examples of well-proportioned furniture, and are admirable for a room designed for men. The room has functioned for planning purposes during three wars: President Lincoln used it for strategic discussions during the Civil War; President McKinley followed the progress of the Spanish-American War, and Winston Churchill (who visited the White House many times during World War II) placed his maps on the walls.

The Grant clock was bought on November 9, 1869, for $500. It is in marble and malachite and shows the day, week, month, and phases of the moon. When the clock was brought to his attention in 1955, President Eisenhower had it repaired and placed in his office. Mrs Kennedy brought it into the Treaty Room.

One interesting feature of the desk marks it as a practical piece of men's furniture. There is a center beam underneath spanning the length of the desk. At specific intervals the beam has been covered in leather, thus protecting it from American men who like to put their feet on the furniture.

Mrs Kennedy sees the room in terms of future needs of the White House. The President sees it as an example of America's history. A moment after the dialogue quoted above, the President entered the room.

(*President Kennedy enters and is seated*)

MR COLLINGWOOD

Mr President, Mrs Kennedy has been showing us about the White House and the changes that she has made therein. What do you think of the changes?

PRESIDENT KENNEDY

Well, I think the great effort that she's made has been to bring us much more intimately in contact with all the men who lived

229

here. After all history is people—and particularly in great moments of our history, Presidents. So when we have, as we do today, Grant's table, Lincoln's bed, Monroe's gold set, all these make these men more alive. I think it makes the White House a stronger panorama of our great story.

MR COLLINGWOOD

Do you mind living in a house that has as many visitors as this one has?

PRESIDENT KENNEDY

Well last year we had the largest in history which I think shows that the White House is becoming more and more important to American people. Over 1,300,000 people passed through our home—but I'd like to see that number doubled this year. What is particularly interesting is that at least two-thirds of them were young school boys and girls. I have always felt that American history is sometimes a dull subject. There's so much emphasis on dates. But I think if they can come here and see alive this building and—in a sense—touch the people who have been here, then they'll go home more interested. I think that they'll become better Americans. Some of them may want to someday live here themselves—which I think would be very good—even the girls.

MR COLLINGWOOD

Well certainly there is a great deal for them to see. Do you, living here as you do, have the same lively sense of the past and of history that those of us who visit this house do?

PRESIDENT KENNEDY

Oh yes, I think even more. In the Executive Wing, which you didn't visit, I sit at a desk which was given by Queen Victoria to Presi-

230

dent Hayes and was used by many of our Presidents. The whole atmosphere touches the lives of these men who led our nation in very difficult times. Of course I think anyone who comes to the White House as a President desires the best for his country, but I think he does receive stimulus from the knowledge of living in close proximity to the people who seem legendary but who actually were alive and who were in these rooms.

MR COLLINGWOOD
You feel then that history can be helpful to understanding the present?

PRESIDENT KENNEDY
Yes, but history isn't a guide to the present. In the Archives Building down Pennsylvania Avenue there's a stone plaque which says "What is past is prologue." While it doesn't give us a key to the future I think it does give us a sense of confidence in the future. This country has passed through very difficult days, but it has passed through them. It is rather interesting to realize that we are rather an old republic—probably the oldest republic in the world. When we were founded there was a king in France, a czar in Russia, an emperor in Peking. Today all that's been wiped away —and yet this country continues. It makes us feel that we will continue in the future. We represent a long effort, building on the lives of the men and the efforts of the men who were here and of the American people in the past.

I consider history—our history—to be a source of strength to us here in the White House and to all the American people. Anything which dramatizes the great story of the United States—as I think the White House does—is worthy of the closest attention and respect by Americans who live here and who visit here and

231

who are part of our citizenry. That's why I am glad that Jackie is making the effort she's making. I know other First Ladies have done it; and I know that those who come after us will continue to try to make this the center of a sense of American historical life.

MR COLLINGWOOD

Thank you, Mr President.

PRESIDENT KENNEDY

Thank you very much.

MR COLLINGWOOD

And thank you, Mrs Kennedy, for showing us this wonderful house and all the wonderful things you're bringing into it.

In the final, edited version of the program, it appeared as if the President entered the Treaty Room, sat down and immediately answered Mr Collingwood's questions. However, there was a brief delay. There had been no time to equip the President with a microphone similar to that used by Mrs Kennedy. While the lights and cameras were being positioned he outlined the trend of his remarks.

The President had just finished a televised press conference, and his delivery in the Treaty Room was sharp and pointed. Later that evening, after he had seen Mrs Kennedy's tour, he requested an opportunity to re-record his statements. The scene was shot again the following morning. The President's remarks were almost the same but his delivery was better attuned to the mood which his wife had set.

233

"Some of them may want to someday live here themselves . . . even the girls."
from President Kennedy's remarks.

234

It was done: the photography was finished. At the end of seven hours Mrs Kennedy was fresh, Mr Collingwood was relieved, and a month of intense technical work faced the CBS News teams.

235

BEHIND THE SCENES

There are no illusions or dreams in the control truck. This equipment has seen every major event in television and these technicians have a chilling honesty. They were the first to know that the program would work properly. "It's a good set and a good star" was the comment.

238

ATour of the White House with Mrs John F. Kennedy was not a costly television program nor a major logistical effort. Compared to the coverage of an election or a space-shoot, the equipment moved into the White House was not a great amount. The final cost of the program was in the neighborhood of $130,000. This sum is equivalent to that spent on a major song-and-dance program, and only slightly more than the run-of-the-week mystery hour. The cost also included special charges required by the fact that Mrs Kennedy's tour appeared on three television networks. Had it appeared on only one, the budget would have been less than $100,000.

Though this figure is modest, it is not the result of parsimoniousness. No restrictions were placed on the amount which could be spent. The production team was specifically told it could expend whatever was necessary for the best possible production. The basic problem was artistic, and could not be solved by a large outlay of cash, nor by an excessive amount of television equipment. The reader may be interested in a professional analysis of a problem in television whose solution has attracted a good deal of attention in a small world of producers, directors, and technicians. As a corollary, some further light may be shed on this exposition of lives and times in the White House.

The problem was simply stated in an early letter from the production team to Miss Pamela Turnure, press secretary to Mrs Kennedy. "A beautiful woman is to discuss line and form. How will it be possible to have the careful photography necessarily dictated by beauty and history—and still preserve the authenticity and enthusiasm of a non-professional?"

At first glance this may seem like an abstract problem of interest to a small group of television executives. But its solution was the key to the broadcast. The rest was minor. Relations with the White House, logistics, inter-network bargaining and research into the history of the building were all capable of solution, given enough time, love, and money.

The producers had to choose between three tools: direct, live, "remote" broadcasting; film; and videotape recording. Each has its own esthetic logic.

Film could be discarded at once. For technical reasons an enormous amount of lighting would have to be moved into the White House, and filming would require at least three days of Mrs Kennedy's time. A non-professional could

239

not sustain the same level of performance over a three-day period, particularly if she were to carry the whole program alone.

Direct, live, "remote" broadcasting was at the other end of the spectrum. Direct broadcasting best fits a story whose ending is not known before the program begins. A baseball game, a political convention, or a space-shoot can only be covered in this manner, and are the best examples of the esthetics of live broadcasting. In 1952, before the invention of videotape recording, President Truman used live broadcasting to show his renovations in the White House. This program was carefully studied, and this type of broadcasting was rejected on the basis that the spontaneity of the photography could not match the artistry of the objects in the White House, nor the story Mrs Kennedy wished to tell.

Videotape recording was the only answer. The plan was to do the program in segments. Each five or six minutes of the broadcast were rehearsed and then photographed immediately afterward. Each room was to be considered a scene. Each scene was to be recorded, and then joined together in a tape editing room at a later date. Before and after Mrs Kennedy appeared, the objects she discussed were to be carefully lit and photographed, and these subscenes were to be inserted into the master tape. The great advantage of videotaping was that Mrs Kennedy would not be under the pressure of live broadcasting, and all technical arrangements could be made to photograph her and record her comments as she made them.

The great danger of videotape is that if it is handled incorrectly all spontaneity is lost. An over-edited tape has neither the precision of a filmed broadcast nor the liveliness of direct transmission. There is no more lively controversy in professional television circles than the degree of editing permissible in a videotaped broadcast. It was this narrow area of technique which excited professional attention.

This "start-and-stop" technique was vitally necessary if Mrs Kennedy were to maintain an uninhibited performance. There is a crude rule of thumb by which professionals reckon the performance of amateurs: a non-professional's performance is at its peak the first or second time he says his piece. Rehearsal and repetition tend to diminish his intensity and believability, and lead to rapid physical and emotional fatigue.

Perhaps an example will clarify the technique.

The day before Mrs Kennedy appeared in the Red Room, all lights and cameras were moved to the north side of the room. This would be the point-of-view of Mrs Kennedy as she entered. The room was photographed from the north in a wide-angle shot. Immediately afterward the lights and cameras were shifted to the south side of the room, to await Mrs Kennedy's entrance.

An example of an unsolved television problem: the cameraman cannot raise his camera high enough to shoot directly into the best features of the Gilbert Stuart portrait. He must tilt his camera and shoot up at Washington's face, thus emphasizing and foreshortening the details. Nothing replaces a visit to the White House.

It was also a struggle to get low angle shots. Special camera mounts were brought from New York. Furniture would only look distinguished when photographed from below eye level.

The production assistant was graciously given a desk by the guard who is stationed under the North Portico.

Additionally, specific objects such as the Lannuier table and the Nellie Custis sofa were shot in careful closeups and placed aside. A stand-in for Mrs Kennedy walked through the room, and small pieces of green tape were placed on the floor.

When Mrs Kennedy arrived, she walked through the room and was shown the suggested positions at which she might stop. She and Mr Collingwood discussed the objects of interest in a single rehearsal, and the scene was immediately photographed and recorded. No attempt was made to photograph closeups of individual objects. The master tape consisted of a long shot and closeups of the First Lady, taken from the north side of the room. The photographs from the south side, and detailed closeups of the artifacts were inserted later.

In this manner both requirements were met. Mrs Kennedy was free to discuss and improvise around any object or subject which came to her mind. Yet careful, detailed photography could be carried out before or after her appearance. Both spontaneity and precision were possible.

Parenthetically, the Red Room sequence was one of the few which had to be shot a second time. The First Lady confused the Nellie Custis sofa with the Dolley Madison divan, and asked to repeat her performance. Additionally, the White House staff had built a roaring, crackling fire. The popping noises interfered with the microphones, and it was necessary to wait until the room was quiet.

Although the final tape had the appearance of a spontaneous broadcast, there were 190 splices in the master tape: this means that 95 scenes or subscenes were inserted.

At the same time that the technical plans were being discussed, intensive research was made into the history of the building. Close liaison was maintained in Washington between the curatorial staff of the White House and the researchers for the television program. The place of every object in every room was drawn on large scale replicas of the White House. A torrent of historical information was gathered together. This book is itself based on the notes supplied during the production period.

It was not the purpose of the production team to write a final text for Mrs Kennedy. But it was assumed that the normal anxieties of space and time might be relieved by completely written texts. The manuscripts gave Mrs Kennedy an idea of how much might be said in each room and still meet the restrictions of a one hour program. (It might be added that the final transcript resembled these scripts only in the sequence of the rooms, and some obviously parallel information. Mrs Kennedy did her own homework and provided information not covered by the manuscripts.)

243

The director briefs the technical crew. The neckties were unexpected. The technical discussion was rapid, thorough, and in the jargon peculiar to television. A White House usher followed the production team through two rooms and then remarked, "I know it's English, but I can't understand five consecutive words!"

Between shots the production team found moments to make private judgments on the President's house.

244

The only meeting between Mrs Kennedy and the production staff was a short conference of fifteen minutes on the day before her appearance. It was felt that careful staff work and pre-planning were more important than a series of script conferences which might lead to nervousness on everyone's part. All details were handled by correspondence.

Since the White House is a public building, there were restrictions on the amount of time the production team could spend in the house. The major effort would begin on a Saturday, just after the White House was closed to tourists. The Executive Mansion is normally closed from noon on Saturday until noon on Tuesday. The estimate was that all work could be done during this time, but several hours were required on Tuesday afternoon to remove the equipment.

Early on Saturday morning, January 13, 1962, fifty-four members of the television crew moved into the White House. Lights, cameras, and cables were put into place. The general plan had been discussed down to minute details. But some unusual events began to take place.

One by one the technicians disappeared—and reappeared wearing neckties. This was a minor, but astounding phenomenon. The technicians understood something that had been lost by the planning staff. This was the White House. The thin edge of the sense of pride began to slide into the production.

The feeling would grow for the next three days. One cameraman had made a serious study of the administration of President Polk, and during a break in the work explained to another that Polk was "one of the most underrated Presidents of the nineteenth century." Others would take advantage of an off-duty moment and sit quietly in the Lincoln Room or the Green Room. Everything was handled with gentleness and care, but the sentiment was covered by a wisecrack or a joke. The stage manager sat at the lavish table of the State Dining Room looking at the Healy portrait of Lincoln—yet when an usher came up to talk to him, the stage manager quipped "Separate checks, please."

The first camera to go into position was placed on the south lawn. The lenses had not yet been placed into the camera when word was given that the President would be departing by helicopter from the lawn. The technicians retreated a respectful distance; the helicopter landed and the presidential aides brought the weekend luggage into the aircraft. Somehow the lens case was placed on board, and the President of the United States flew away with the equipment.

The Kennedy family spent Saturday and Sunday in Virginia. The television crews shot all the planned sequences, and reassembled Monday morning for the principal photography involving Mrs Kennedy.

245

Outside the White House were the impersonal machines of television—

—inside the building every effort was made to keep the technical problems away from Mrs Kennedy.

Late in the afternoon. The East Sitting Hall on the second floor. By this time Mrs Kennedy was acclimated to the television crew and the television crew was used to her.

247

A number of contingency plans were in the background. All depended on Mrs Kennedy's performance and strength. Scene I, Take I, was to be a long walk from the East Executive Wing through the corridor on the ground floor, and a short interview in the Curator's Office. The success of this scene would indicate the shooting pattern for the rest of the day.

No retakes were necessary. It was obvious that her intensity about the White House and her work was communicable. The basic premise of non-fictional television was proved again: the amateur could do what the professional could not.

Everyone concerned with the production has been asked many times: "What's she like?" The question is ambiguous. To the professional, it has a specific meaning. The professional can answer only in terms of performance on a television set. Mrs Kennedy was calm; knew what she wanted to do and say; exhibited a minor and predictable amount of nervousness and was able to disregard almost totally the mechanics of television. It had been decided that only the director and the correspondent would speak to her. The director would suggest her movements through a scene and the correspondent would discuss in advance the editorial content of the scene. The latter was more to motivate his questions than to suggest her responses.

Mrs Kennedy was slightly apprehensive about the number of retakes that might be required, but the recording on the ground floor took less than an hour. Afterward she seemed to enjoy the work. She had forgotten about lunch until reminded and was willing to continue without food. Since the television crew had begun work at seven in the morning, a lunch period was inserted for their benefit.

There had been a great deal of apprehension about damaging the White House with light towers and other technical equipment. In the main corridor traversing the first floor there are two cut glass chandeliers which pre-date the Executive Mansion. As a light tower was being moved from the State Dining Room into the East Room an enormous crash was heard. The producing team was paralyzed.

Someone said, "See if it's ours or theirs."

It was ours: a large light bulb had fallen out of a reflector.

For technical reasons the program was recorded out of sequence. The State Dining Room was photographed before the East Room, but the scenes were reversed when the tape was edited. This out-of-sequence shooting did not disturb Mrs Kennedy, and the shooting of the first floor was completed ahead of schedule. The second floor was also shot in inverse order. The President had agreed to make an appearance, but his schedule was such that the end of the broadcast was photographed before the penultimate scene.

The President's scene was shot quickly; too quickly for his taste, as it later developed. He had prepared a page of notes which he studied, discussed briefly with Mr Collingwood, and then recorded. Mr Kennedy arrived from a press conference where the rhythm of questions and responses was not the same as the more leisurely pace of the broadcast. Later that night, when the tapes were replayed for him and Mrs Kennedy, the President requested that he be permitted to do his scene again. The editorial content of his second performance was the same, but his mood better fit the pacing which Mrs Kennedy had set.

At seven o'clock on Monday night Mrs Kennedy had finished all scenes which involved photography of her. She asked to see the rough-cut tapes which were presented on a television set in the private theater. She made a few notes suggesting changes. A week later an audio crew recorded a narration which was fitted to historical photographs of the White House and to photographs of paintings acquired for the building.

Three weeks were spent in editing the tapes, recording music, and preparing the program for broadcast. Mrs Kennedy did not ask to review the finished program. CBS News requested that her press secretary, Miss Pamela Turnure, be made available for comments and suggestions. A few technical errors were corrected and the program was ready for broadcast.

It is estimated that 80,000,000 Americans saw the program. Additionally, the broadcast has been transmitted in many European and Asian countries. The United States Information Service is distributing the program throughout the world. It has been called "one of the great landmarks" of American television and has been placed in the governmental archives.

Some 10,000 letters have been received from school children, ordinary citizens and national leaders. The subsidiary result has been that the lines of tourists have all but doubled at the North Gate of the White House. It will take sixty years for the same number of people to see the building as saw the television program.

Yet the television program was a minor footnote in the life of the White House.

The basic theme of this book has been that the White House reflects the life of America. No one event can have more meaning than the history of this building. The story of the President's house has been written by great and small men and great and small events. Some treasures that should have remained in the building have been lost: some minute details have clung tenaciously, despite the waves of redecoration and the tides of history. A television program recorded seven hours in the life of this building: the story stretches out far longer, both before and after.

249

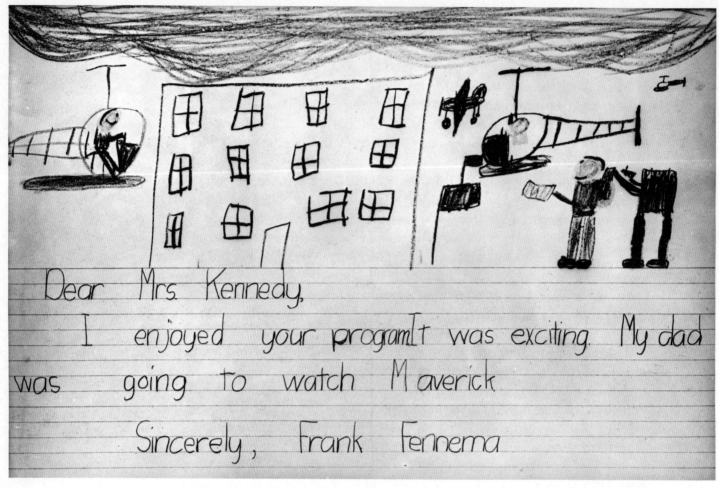

Dear Mrs. Kennedy,
I enjoyed your program It was exciting. My dad was going to watch Maverick.
Sincerely, Frank Fennema

Mrs Kennedy received many letters from children.

Bibliography

ADAMS, HENRY, *Democracy,* Greenwich, Conn., Fawcett Publications, Inc., 1961.

ADAMS, JAMES TRUSLOW, *The Adams Family,* New York, Hillary House, Inc., 1957.

ANTHONY, KATHERINE SUSAN, *Dolly Madison,* Garden City, N.Y., Doubleday & Co., 1959.

ARONSON, JOSEPH, *The Book of Furniture & Decoration,* New York, Crown Publishing Co., 1936.

BOULANGER, GISELE, *l'Art de Reconnaitre les Styles,* Paris, Librarie Hachette, 1960.

BROWN, GLEN, *1860-1930, Memories,* Washington, W. F. Roberts Co., 1931.

BROWN, MARGARET, *Dresses of the First Ladies of the White House,* Washington, Smithsonian Institution, 1952.

CAEMMERER, HANS P., *Manual on Origin & Development of Washington,* Washington, U.S. Government Printing Office, 1939.

CARPENTER, FRANK G., *Carp's Washington,* New York, McGraw-Hill, 1960.

COSTANTINO, RUTH, *How to Know French Antiques,* New York, New American Library, 1961.

CRESSON, W. P., *James Monroe,* Chapel Hill, N.C., University of North Carolina Press, 1946.

CROOK, W. H., *Memories of the White House,* Boston, Little, Brown & Co., 1911.

DREPPERD, CARL W., *The Primer of American Antiques,* New York, Doubleday, Doran & Co., 1945.

DULLES, FOSTER RHEA, *The U.S. Since 1865,* Ann Arbor, University of Michigan Press, 1959.

DUPEE, F. W., *Henry James,* Garden City, Doubleday & Co., Inc., 1956.

EBERLEIN, H. and HUBBARD, C., *Historic Houses of Georgetown & Washington,* Richmond, Va., The Dietz Press, Inc.

EISEN, GUSTAVIUS A., *Portraits of Washington,* New York, R. Hamilton & Associates, 1932.

FIELDS, ALONZO, *My 21 Years in the White House,* New York, Coward-McCann, Inc., 1960.

FRARY, IHNA T., *Thomas Jefferson, Architect and Builder,* Richmond, Va., Garret & Massie, 1950.

FRICK ART REFERENCE LIBRARY, *Paintings in the White House,* edited by Katharine McCook Knox.

FURMAN, BESS, *White House Profile,* Indianapolis, New York, Bobbs-Merrill Co., Inc., 1951.

GOLENPAUL, DAN, *Information Please Almanac 1962,* New York, Simon and Schuster, 1962.

HAGEDORN, HERMANN, *The Roosevelt Family of Sagamore Hill,* New York, The Macmillan Co., 1954.

HAMILTON, HOLMAN, *White House Images & Realities*, Gainesville, University of Florida Press, 1958.

HELLER, DEAN & DAVID, *Jacqueline Kennedy,* Derby, Conn., Monarch Books, Inc., 1961.

HELM, EDITH, *The Captains and the Kings*, New York, G. P. Putnam & Sons, 1954.

HOLLOWAY, LAURA, *The Ladies of the White House*, New York, U.S. Publishing Co., 1870.

HOOVER, IRWIN, *Forty-two Years in the White House*, Boston, Houghton, Mifflin Co., 1934.

HURD, CHARLES, *The White House*, New York, Harper & Bros., 1940.

JAFFRAY, ELIZABETH, *Secrets of the White House,* New York, Cosmopolitan Book Corp., 1927.

JEFFRIES, ONA GRIFFIN, *In and Out of the White House*, New York, Wilfred Funk, Inc., 1960.

JENSEN, AMY LA FOLLETTE, *The White House & Its 32 Families*, New York, McGraw-Hill, 1958.

JOHNSTON, FRANCES B., *The White House*, Washington, Gibson Bros., 1893.

KRAUS, MICHAEL, *The U.S. to 1865*, Ann Arbor, University of Michigan Press, 1959.

LATROBE, BENJAMIN, *The Journal of Latrobe*, New York, D. Appleton, 1905.

LEECH, MARGARET, *Reveille in Washington,* New York, Harper & Bros., 1941.

LEEMING, JOSEPH, *The White House in Picture and Story,* New York, G. W. Stewart Publishing Co., Inc., 1953.

LINDSAY, C. H. FORBES, *Washington—The City and the Seat of Government*, Philadelphia, John C. Winston Co., 1908.

LONGWORTH, ALICE ROOSEVELT, *Crowded Hours*, New York, Charles Scribner & Sons, 1933.

LOOKER, EARLE, *The White House Gang*, New York, Fleming H. Revell Co., 1929.

MCCONNELL, JANE & BURT, *Our First Ladies*, New York, Thomas Y. Crowell Co., 1953.

MORGAN, JAMES, *Our Presidents*, New York, The Macmillan Co., 1958.

MORRIS, EDWIN BATEMAN, *Report of the Commission on the Renovation of the Executive Mansion,* U.S. Government Printing Office, 1952.

PARKS, LILLIAN, *My 30 Years Backstairs at the White House,* New York, Fleet Publishing Corp., 1961.

RANDALL, RUTH PAINTER, *Mary Lincoln*, Boston, Little, Brown & Co., 1953.

ROOSEVELT, ELEANOR, *This I Remember*, New York, Harper & Bros., 1949.

ROOSEVELT, JAMES, *Affectionately, F.D.R.*, New York, Avon Book Division, Hearst Corp., 1959.

ROSS, ISABEL, *Grace Coolidge and Her Era*, New York, Dodd, Mead & Co., 1962.

SCHLESINGER, ARTHUR, JR., *The Age of Jackson*, Boston, Little, Brown & Co., 1953.

SMITH, MARGARET BAYARD, *The First 40 Years of Washington Society,* Letters edited by Gaillard Hunt, New York, Charles Scribner & Sons, 1906.

SWEETSER, KATE D., *Famous Girls of the White House*, Revised Edition, New York, Thomas Y. Crowell Co., 1937.

Bibliography

Train, Arthur, Jr., *The Story of Everyday Things*, New York, Harper & Bros., 1941.

Truett, Randle B., *The White House*, New York, Hastings House, 1949.

Truman, Margaret, *Souvenir*, New York, McGraw-Hill, 1956.

Tully, Andrew, *The Day They Burnt the White House*, New York, Simon and Schuster, 1961.

Willets, Gilson, *Inside History of the White House*, New York, Christian Herald, 1908.

Wilson, Edith, *My Memoir*, Indianapolis, New York, Bobbs-Merrill Co., 1939.

Picture Credits

Library of Congress, Prints and Photographs: pages 14, 17 (bottom), 21, 23, 24, 25, 27, 43, 66, 67, 70, 71, 73, 74, 75, 76, 88, 89, 91, 92, 93, 94, 95, 96, 105, 115, 116, 117, 118, 119, 120, 140, 141, 159, 160, 184 (right), 188, 189, 191 (left), 196, 207, 208, 215, 223.

Library of Congress, Manuscript Division: page 121

National Park Service, U.S. Department of Interior: pages 17 (center), 28, 31, 33, 35, 36, 60, 77, 87, 162 (left), 170, 211.

The White House: pages 56, 57, 58, 59, color following 98, color following 192.

National Archives and Records: pages 122, 150.

Frick Art Reference Library: pages 162 (bottom right), 169 (right), 175, 178, 183 (left), 184 (left).

Maryland Historical Society: page 17 (top).

Pennsylvania Academy of the Fine Arts: page 165.

Harris and Ewing: pages 198, 201.

United Press International: page 191.

Mrs. Edythe McGinnis: page 136.

Smithsonian Institution: page 114, 223.

Wildenstein Gallery: page 149.

All others CBS.

Picture Credits

All photographs of Mrs Kennedy in the modern White House were taken by William Warnecke, and most of the turn-of-the-century photographs are the work of Frances Benjamin Johnston, one of the first women to use a camera professionally.

Mr Warnecke belongs to a distinguished family of famous news photographers: his father was one of the first press photographers in New York City. William Warnecke's work for the Columbia Broadcasting System has covered the field, from formal portraits to spot news. He has photographed four Presidents, from Franklin Roosevelt to John Kennedy. The assignment given to Mr Warnecke was difficult—he was to photograph Mrs Kennedy and the White House only during dress rehearsal. Since the First Lady was so completely prepared, there were often no formal rehearsals of individual scenes, and the photographer had to make many of the pictures in this book during the taping of the program. He could not use flash-bulbs or lights of his own and he had to be aware of the quick movements of television cameras, as well as Mrs Kennedy's detailed stage movements. Above all, he was not to concentrate so fully on his assignment as to risk being discovered by the electronic cameras. Nevertheless he turned out a series of pictures which has been called "the most distinguished news photography of the White House in recent years." Mr Warnecke lives in Crestwood, New York, with his wife and four children.

Frances Benjamin Johnston wrote to George Eastman about 1880, "Please send a camera which will take good pictures for newspapers."

The beginning of her career echoes Jacqueline Bouvier Kennedy. Miss Johnston was a pretty photographer, and in time became the unofficial pictorial reporter of the White House. She photographed the building during the administrations of Harrison, Cleveland, McKinley, Theodore Roosevelt, and Taft.

Her work at the White House led to commissions to photograph old houses throughout the nation. Her collection of portraits of famous American houses numbered over 1000 by 1932, and Frances Johnston became a standard photographic authority in the field of architecture. In November 1945 she was the first woman to become an honorary member of the American Institute of Architects. In 1948 she presented her collection of famous photographs to the Library of Congress. She died in 1952.

Almost all of the pictures credited to the National Park Service were taken by Mr Abbie Rowe who has had a long and distinguished career as the official White House photographer.

254

Index

255

256

The Presidents of
The United States of America

PRESIDENTS	INAUGURATION DATES
George Washington	1789
John Adams	1797
Thomas Jefferson	1801
James Madison	1809
James Monroe	1817
John Quincy Adams	1825
Andrew Jackson	1829
Martin Van Buren	1837
William Henry Harrison	1841
John Tyler	1841
James K. Polk	1845
Zachary Taylor	1849
Millard Fillmore	1850
Franklin Pierce	1853
James Buchanan	1857
Abraham Lincoln	1861
Andrew Johnson	1865
Ulysses S. Grant	1869
Rutherford B. Hayes	1877
James A. Garfield	1881
Chester A. Arthur	1881
Grover Cleveland	1885
Benjamin Harrison	1889
Grover Cleveland	1893
William McKinley	1897
Theodore Roosevelt	1901
William Howard Taft	1909
Woodrow Wilson	1913
Warren G. Harding	1921
Calvin Coolidge	1923
Herbert C. Hoover	1929
Franklin D. Roosevelt	1933
Harry S. Truman	1945
Dwight D. Eisenhower	1953
John F. Kennedy	1961